The Accidental Feminist

"Courtney Reissig is a true daughter of Sarah. She is wise, discerning, brave, and thoughtful. This book is a needed antidote to the false views of women we so often encounter, and too often absorb, in our culture."

Russell D. Moore, President, The Ethics & Religious Liberty Commission; author, *Tempted and Tried*

"*The Accidental Feminist* reminds me of a handbook on womanhood, but not a rule book. Courtney shares the beautiful design of all aspects of women made in the image of God. A perfect read for anyone desiring to gain an understanding of womanhood in the Bible."

Trillia Newbell, author, *United: Captured by God's Vision for Diversity* and *Fear and Faith*

"Courtney writes as a daughter of third-wave feminism who is calling her sisters to return to God's instructions for how we should live as Christian women in a fallen world. This book unveils what has been lost in our hearts, our relationships, and our churches. It exposes the 'options' feminism offers as just a set of heavy shackles designed to hold us back from seeking fulfillment in the only place it can really be found—in the hope of the gospel of Christ."

Kristie Anyabwile, wife of Thabiti Anyabwile, Assistant Pastor for Church Planting, Capitol Hill Baptist Church, Washington, DC; mom of three; discipler of women

"Over the past few decades, we've unwittingly absorbed popular ideas about womanhood. We've become feminists without knowing it. Courtney challenges us to wake from the stupor. If you're a young woman, you would do well to read this book and consider whether you, too, have become an accidental feminist."

Mary A. Kassian, Professor of Women's Studies, The Southern Baptist Theological Seminary; author, *Girls Gone Wise in a World Gone Wild*

"Courtney Reissig has written what is sure to become the standard guide to Christian womanhood in a feminist age. Her book is practical, winsome, and full of rich theology. It is particularly strong—and unusual—because the content rests alongside a powerful narrative of personal transformation. Like the Savior it extols, this is a book that is going to strengthen, unsettle, and ultimately bless many readers—and there is nothing accidental about that."

Owen D. Strachan, Assistant Professor of Christian Theology and Church History, Boyce College; President, The Council on Biblical Manhood and Womanhood

"Thoughtful and authentic, Courtney Reissig masterfully uncovers the struggles women have in discovering their identity and purpose. She presents a thorough picture of feminism and the confusion it has wrought regarding the roles of women today and the definition of 'equality.' She reveals the true liberation women can experience as they embrace a biblical view of womanhood. Regardless of age or background, *The Accidental Feminist* is a book every woman should read!"

Monica Rose Brennan, Associate Professor and Director of Women's Ministries, Liberty University

"Being female isn't just a category; it's a good gift written in our DNA by a Creator who loves us and is for us. Courtney Reissig affirms this truth from Scripture as well as her own story. Her journey from resisting her design to embracing it with joy is a faithful guide for young Christian women wondering what to make of being female. In a day when *male* and *female* are seen as too confining, when it is said that gender is best bent to the whims of our personal expression, Reissig faithfully shows why being made female, in the image of God, is an exceedingly good gift."

Candice Watters, Assistant Editor, CMBW.org's Family Channel; cofounder, Boundless.org; coauthor, *Start Your Family*

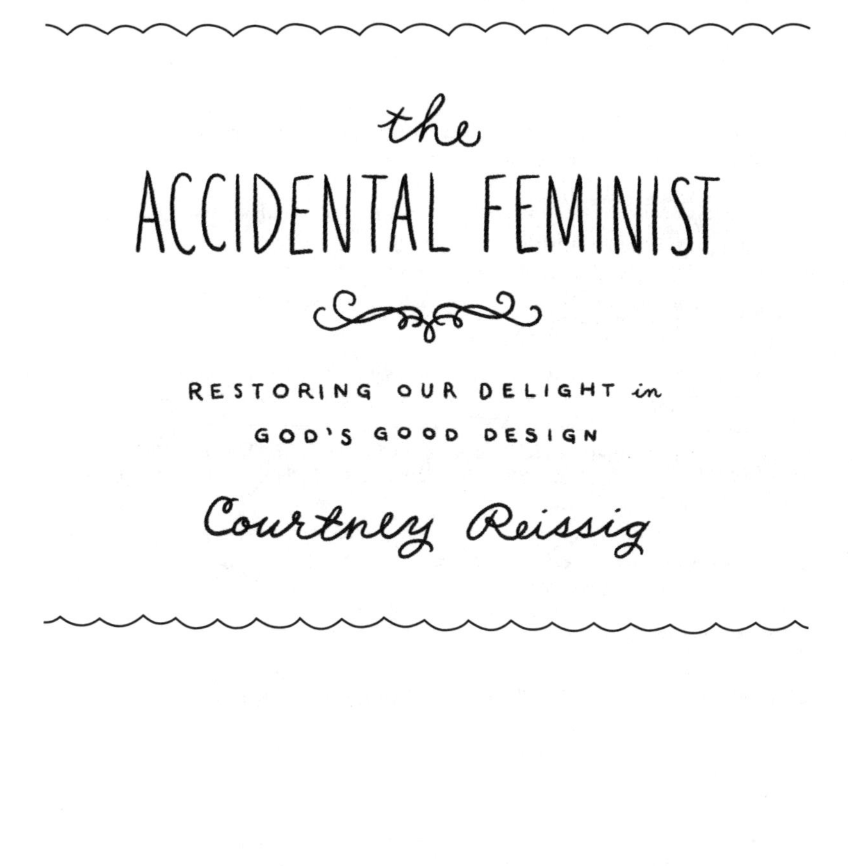

WHEATON, ILLINOIS

The Accidental Feminist: Restoring Our Delight in God's Good Design

Published by Crossway
1300 Crescent Street
Wheaton, Illinois 60187

Published in association with the literary agency of Wolgemuth & Associates, Inc.

Cover design: Connie Gabbert

Cover image: Sunny Studio/Shutterstock

First printing 2015

Printed in the United States of America

All emphases in Scripture quotations have been added by the author.

Trade paperback ISBN: 978-1-4335-4548-1
ePub ISBN: 978-1-4335-4551-1
PDF ISBN: 978-1-4335-4549-8
Mobipocket ISBN: 978-1-4335-4550-4

Library of Congress Cataloging-in-Publication Data

Reissig, Courtney, 1983–
The accidental feminist : restoring our delight in God's good design / Courtney Reissig.
pages cm
Includes bibliographical references and index.
ISBN 978-1-4335-4548-1 (tp)—ISBN 978-1-4335-4551-1 (ePub)—
ISBN 978-1-4335-4550-4 (Mobipocket)
1. Women—Religious aspects—Christianity. 2. Feminism—Religious aspects—Christianity. I. Title.
BT704.R45 2015
233'.5—dc23 2015007574

Crossway is a publishing ministry of Good News Publishers.

VP 25 24 23 22 21 20 19 18 17 16 15
15 14 13 12 11 10 9 8 7 6 5 4 3 2 1

To Daniel,
my best friend, my greatest
supporter, and the love of my life.
Thank you for loving this accidental feminist.

Contents

Acknowledgments

Whenever I buy a book, I always turn to the acknowledgments page first. Call me sentimental, but I like to see how the relationships of the author aided his or her writing process. My story is no different. It took a mighty village to get this book to paper. In fact, this book wouldn't have been an idea if Owen Strachan had not planted the seed in my mind nearly four years ago. So thank you for the nudge, Owen. I would never have thought this book were possible if it weren't for my wonderful agent, Erik Wolgemuth, and the entire team of Wolgemuth & Associates. Thank you for believing in my writing and working so hard for the book's publication. My editors Dave DeWit and Tara Davis were a tremendous encouragement throughout the entire writing and editing process. If you read anything helpful in this book, it is owing to their editing expertise.

God faithfully provided dear friends and family who were willing to read early chapters of the book and give needed feedback and critique. Thank you Katelyn Beaty, Megan Hill, Katie Van Dyke, Emily Tarter, and my parents, Rick and Deb Tarter, for reading portions (or all) of the book. And no acknowledgment could even begin to express how thankful I am for my dear friend, Laura Breeding. She carefully read every chapter and helped make it better than it ever would have been without her insight. Laura, your friendship and wisdom are invaluable to me.

Writers never write in isolation. Writing is a collaborative experience, and I am blessed by writer friends who sharpen and challenge me to think and write clearly and biblically. Thank you to my fellow Her.meneutics writers who have been my cheerleaders in life and writing. I am so blessed to call you friends. And thank you to my dear friend and fellow CBMW editor, Trillia Newbell. Your friendship these last few years has meant the world to me.

Marriage is a partnership of equals. I am blessed to experience such a partnership with my husband, Daniel. He is my greatest friend, my greatest supporter, and my greatest love. He provided me with space and time to write and has talked through (or listened to me talk through) every aspect of this book over the course of our marriage. Thank you, babe, for loving me and encouraging me to write. I could not do this without your support. This book is one piece of the journey of our life together. I pray for many more years to the journey.

And finally, to my precious twin boys, Luke and Zach, while you may not fully comprehend the words of this book for many, many years, I pray even now that you will grow to be men who love God's Word and his design for you as men. You bring me more joy than I ever knew possible, and it has made all of the years I waited for you worth it. I would wait a million more if it meant I could have you as my sons.

The prevailing theme in my life throughout the writing of this book was unexpected weakness. All I can do is praise God for his grace. This book is a testimony of his strength in my weakness. All glory goes to him alone.

Introduction

I'm an Accidental Feminist

My name is Courtney. I am an accidental feminist.

I never burned my bra or anything, and I liked boys way too much to completely write them off as useless. But for many years I unwittingly possessed some heart attitudes that made me a classic feminist. And I've met many other accidental feminists, both inside and outside the church.

You might be reading this book because you proudly identify yourself with card-carrying feminists. Maybe you think feminism and Christianity aren't mutually exclusive. Welcome, this book is for you.

On the other hand, you might be a Christian woman who is skeptical every time you see the word *feminist*. You want to learn more about what it means to grow as a woman who follows Christ, and you don't really think *feminist* describes you. In fact, in some of your circles *feminist* is a dirty word reserved only for women who do not want a husband or who volunteer at Planned Parenthood. Feminism is most certainly not in your conservative church. This book is for you too.

Or maybe you aren't a skeptic or a feminist. You simply want to learn what it means to be a godly woman in these confusing days. Yes, this book is for you too.

Some Christians define feminism as simply equality among the sexes. For them, feminism means men and women are equal. As one writer puts it: "At the core, feminism simply consists of the radical notion that women are people, too."[1] The reality is that feminism is hard to pin down. As the culture has evolved, so has the concept of feminism. We will explore that evolution throughout this book. As postmodernism has taken root in our psyches, the definition of feminism can now mean anything you want it to mean. In fact, as I was writing this introduction, the media was blasting a celebrity for refusing to define herself as a feminist because, as she put it, "I like men." Some in the media were appalled that she defined feminism so loosely or that she seemed to completely brush off the label. Others acknowledged that to be a feminist today means different things for different people.[2] This is not your grandmother's feminism.

For our purposes I am going to define feminism as *equality equals sameness*. I hope you will see what I mean.

Regardless of where you're coming from, I pray you will find yourself right at home. I know what it's like to embrace feminism with all of its promises of freedom and independence. I know what it's like to struggle with feminism—to learn about but not fully adopt its ideas, thinking that there might be something more to the path of being a godly woman. I also know what it's like to think that feminism no longer has an effect on me. I know what it's like to want to be a godly woman while being bombarded with images and influences urging me to be the exact opposite.

"But I'm Not a Feminist"

But what if the whole independence deal doesn't appeal to you at all? Maybe you haven't struggled with feminism like I did. You might look at feminism and wisely see the baggage it brings to our understanding of womanhood and want nothing to do with it. Many women have this perspective. With the rise of feminism in the 1970s came the countering rise of the biblical womanhood movement. Women like Susan Hunt, Mary Kassian, and Nancy Leigh DeMoss faithfully taught (and continue to teach) God's Word on womanhood and stood against the culture's influence. By God's grace, godly women saw what was happening in the culture and sought to live against the fast-moving waters of feminism and independence. But like so many good things, over the years in some circles the definition of *womanhood* has moved from an earnest desire to be different and godly to a list of tasks that even the Proverbs 31 woman couldn't complete.

It's interesting that even outside of the church, younger women are rebelling against the feminism of their mothers. It used to be considered "letting down the team" if a woman chose to stay home with her children rather than launch back into the workplace after her pregnancy. Now many moms are either chucking the career altogether or looking for more flexible options so they can spend the majority of their time with their children.

If we really want to develop our understanding of what it means to be a woman, we have to stop rebelling against each passing generation. If we follow the swinging pendulum of ambient culture, the rebellion will shift in another fifty years or so. But if we anchor ourselves to the Word of God, we will be able to withstand the shifting sands of every generational rebellion.

Miss Independent

I believe many women today find themselves confused, just like I was as an early Christian. Part of my rebellion against things that I deemed too domestic or feminine was rooted in my misunderstanding of what it means to be a Christian woman. What exactly does it look like to be a Christian wife? Is it baking cookies, keeping an immaculate home, and being a mom to five kids? What about the woman who is a baking novice or, like me, a baking failure? Is womanhood only about the quiet and sensitive types? What about the woman who has a career? The woman who can't have kids or simply doesn't want a "quiverful"? What about the woman who doesn't feel gifted to teach in her local church? Is there a place for her? What about the woman who does? Does she fit? What about the vast number of single women in our churches today? Is there room for these sisters?

Caricatures of womanhood are what get us into trouble. When we reduce womanhood to the tasks we accomplish, or cultural expectations, or talents and personality traits, we are doing a disservice to women everywhere. Recovering from feminism and embracing God's idea of womanhood is far more than a throwback to a 1950s television show.

Before I grasped the gospel and clung to Christ as my Savior, I was the stereotypical, secular millennial feminist. Marriage was low on my priority list. I thought marriage would only interfere with my desire to do what I wanted, which was to be a big-city writer who dated around and dressed fashionably. Children definitely didn't factor into my equation. In my college literary theory class, I devoured feminist thought, fully believing that every story had an angle dealing with the oppression of women. While I enjoyed dating men, I didn't have much respect for them apart from the companionship and attention they provided me. The thought of being barefoot, pregnant, and permanently joined to a man scared me. It wasn't that I didn't like kids. I actually loved them. And I really liked boys (too much, in fact). My fear was that I would be defined by something other than myself. I wanted freedom and independence. I wanted to have a career. I wanted to do something big with my life. Maybe later I would think about kids and a husband. But in my early twenties, I was focused on me and my goals. I wanted to set the pace for my life, and in my mind a husband and children would only slow me down.

You see, I thought freedom meant independence. Independence from men, the burden of children (when I wasn't ready for them), and ultimately from authority. I didn't want anyone else calling the shots in my life, especially if that someone was a man. I thought I could be free only if I was the one who made the decisions for my life. I wanted choices and options. If I chose marriage and children, fine. But I didn't want another person choosing for me. Lack of independence was akin to being trapped. And I knew I didn't want that for the rest of my life.

What I failed to understand was that true freedom cannot be found in independence from authority at all. True freedom is found in understanding our Creator and how he wants us to live. True freedom is knowing that this world has meaning, and we are created for a purpose. True freedom is knowing that God had a good design when he created us male and female. But it took me a little while to get to the point where I was truly free.

You might hear this part of my story and think, *What's wrong with having goals and wanting to do something with your life? If that's feminism, what's the problem?* I hope you will hang with me.

A Brief History of American Feminism

Feminism started as a movement that aimed to give women options. Good options. At the turn of the twentieth century women couldn't vote, own property, or make independent decisions that many of us take for granted today. It began as a rising up against male authority and male oppression of women. Many of those early feminists were truly oppressed by unfair labor practices and having a limited voice in society. But the movement wasn't just about true oppression, as Carolyn McCulley helpfully asserts in her book *Radical Womanhood: Feminine Faith in a Feminist World*. The *first wave of feminism,* also known as the suffragist movement, cared about additional issues, like the reformation of Christianity and a woman's property rights in marriage.[3] For many first-wave feminists, men were a problem. This attitude led to rebellion.

After the initial issues of first-wave feminism were addressed (such as women securing the right to vote), feminism continued to be defined as personal autonomy and freedom from men. Feminists continued to rebel against cultural expectations of women. In the 1950s and 1960s, the rebellion was against the caricature of the "typical" housewife (think June Cleaver). By the 1970s, women were entering the workforce in droves, demanding equal pay for work, and further seeking to make a mark for themselves as autonomous beings. While some of the advances of *second-wave feminism* were good (equal pay for work, sexual harassment laws in the workplace, etc.), others only widened the dividing line between men and women. Additionally, as feminism of the 70s launched women out of the home and into the workforce, women found purpose and identity outside of a husband and children.

What feminism did was slowly erase the differences between men and women. *Equality now means sameness.* If men and women are truly equal (and I believe they are), then, according to feminism, that equality assumes no distinction in how they live. We've all heard of the saying "anything you can do, I can do better."[4] Women are on equal footing with men and therefore have the right to do anything they can do. If a woman wants to fight in combat, who is to stop her? If a man wants to be a stay-at-home dad, he's met with high fives and praise for his progressive living. If a little girl wants to play on the same football team as her older brothers, we welcome her with open arms. In today's society, the equality of men and women means there are very few differences when it comes to what they can or should do.

Now that equality means sameness, women are ever trying to break the proverbial glass ceiling. Now that equality means sameness, it doesn't matter who's the leader in a relationship. Now that equality means sameness, women have the freedom to excel and achieve in all that men can do. Like so much of the feminist movement, the good that has come out of it is mixed with bad. Women can vote, own property, and have their own credit cards, but that is not all that feminism accomplished for women. The idea that women have complete control over their own lives is what led to the seminal Roe v. Wade case, effectively legalizing abortion-on-demand in America. Like all movements, feminism has had both positive and negative effects.

The feminism of the 70s birthed *third-wave feminism*. In a sort of hyper-rebellion according to the equality-means-sameness notion, this new wave of feminism embraced female sexuality and attempted to use it for women's advantage. This societal movement led to the likes of *Sex and the City,* Miley Cyrus, and the rampant sexuality that we see today. If equality means sameness in feminist thought, then to be equal with men means treating sex like men do, free of emotion and commitment. Or so the thought process goes.

Feminism began as an ideology that promised equality and freedom from the control of men. It has become an ideology that tells women they can use their power, sexuality, and freedom to influence men.

Feminism has gone from a small movement that launched more women into the workforce and gave them the freedom to define themselves to a mainstream ideology that many women are proud to embrace. Ask any woman on the street if she is a feminist and most likely she will either say yes or at least identify strongly with feminist ideals. Feminism is as natural to us as breathing. But we don't always recognize it. Forty years ago women weren't having conversations about leveraging their femininity to get ahead in their careers. Women weren't trying to have a husband, kids, and a growing career all at once like they are now. And they definitely weren't trying to do it all with a smile on their face. Feminism showed women that they had more options. And as their options grew more vast and diverse, so did their desires. It used to be that to be a feminist meant putting off your desire for family and a home life if you were going to make something of yourself. Now it doesn't. Now women truly can "have it all" without giving up their identity. Feminism has become whatever you want it to be. This is why a stay-at-home mom can proudly call herself a feminist just as much as the female executive running a company can. Feminism is so fluid now. But what has stayed the same is the idea that women should have choices. Women should be able to be independent if they want to be. Their lives should not be dictated by culture or stereotypes.

I embraced feminist ideology, not necessarily the feminist movement. I didn't make it my mission to advance feminist causes and see feminism expand in the world, but I did believe in the general premise of feminism. I wanted autonomy. I wanted independence. I can still hear myself telling my college boyfriend, "Don't you tell me what to do. I can make my own decisions." While I had no business listening to him for many other reasons, my point in defying him was that I was a woman and I was my own deciding voice. Again, I thought freedom meant independence. I wanted that freedom. I liked the idea of defining my own identity. I wanted to be the master of my own destiny. This drive for independence was the key aspect of feminism that I bought hook, line, and sinker. As an unbeliever, I believed that depending on a man meant giving up my dreams for a career and future. Even as a new Christian, I held on to this fear. But—as a small concession—I picked a slightly more religious career to pour my energy into. I wanted to do something I defined as meaningful, and keeping a home and raising a family was not on my list of world-changing life goals.

Though my actions and thinking as a young Christian had all the marks of feminism, I wouldn't have labeled myself as a feminist. In fact, if you had asked me if I was a feminist, I probably would have responded with little more than indifference. I knew that I was a feminist preconversion, but I didn't really care once I became a Christian. For many women in my generation, feminism as a movement seems tired and old. It's the movement of a world of yesterday. And that is how feminism has become a part of us. Very few women are talking about being card-carrying feminists today, but the reality is that many women live willfully free from authority. Many women buy into the idea that *equality means sameness*—even if they do so in the slightest of ways. As human beings, we have been fighting authority since the first sin was committed in the garden. And this only makes it harder to submit to the One who has authority over everything—God.

In fact, the more I have gotten to know women my age (in their thirties) and younger, the more I've realized that most of us think feminism is some far-away ideology that doesn't really pertain to us.

Or if we are aware of it, we don't understand how it influences us as Christian women.

A Feminist Where You Least Expect Her

We need to understand a common misconception about feminists. Are you ready for it? Feminist thinking isn't found only outside the church. It's within the church. It's within *my* thinking. It's within yours too.

Maybe you have grown up in the church, and you never once consciously desired independence from men or God. Or maybe you are quite the opposite. You are still in the throes of wrestling through what it means to live as a Christian woman in the wake of your feminist upbringing. Or maybe you are somewhere in the middle, and you don't know exactly what you think.

No matter what your experience, the reality is that everyone has questioned God and his character. We have all wondered if what he has said about us as women, human beings, and image-bearers is true. We have all asked the question, "Did God actually say . . . ?"

Sound familiar? A lady named Eve thought the same thing (Genesis 3). If we are going to make any progress in understanding what it means to be a woman in this crazy world we live in, we must first understand that we come from the same stock.

Since the fall of Adam and Eve, we have been in a battle of the sexes, but—more importantly—we have been in a battle against our Creator. Fast forward to the twenty-first century and we have a full-fledged movement behind us. For those of us born after the 1970s, we don't know a world where "girl power" isn't popular and the culture of hypersexuality is not the norm. Feminism is in our bones now, and many of us do not even know it.

Feminist ideology is not relegated to the brash Gloria Steinem types, or even the female executive with the corner office. Rather, feminism rises up in ordinary women in our congregations, homes, and in the least obvious place, the mirror. Feminism is in the core of our hearts apart from the saving work of the shed blood of Christ, and not simply because we are militant against male authority, but primarily because we are opposed to the greatest authority of all—our Creator. The feminist is not some abstract woman "out there." She is staring at us every morning when we put on our makeup. We are all feminists in need of recovery. We have all shaken our fists at God and wanted something different from his good design for us.

Where We Are Headed

These are weighty matters. These are unpopular matters too. As I was writing this book, I took a short writing retreat to finish a couple of chapters. When I checked into my hotel, the woman at the front desk asked me the customary question to guests: "What brings you to stay with us tonight?"

I froze. I could feel my heart begin to race as I thought how to answer her question. A slew of responses raced through my mind.

"I'm just here on business." Not exactly the truth, but not a lie either.

"I'm just having my first night away from my twin boys." Again, not a lie. But not the full truth.

In the brief moments between her question and my answer, conviction hit me. Perhaps God was giving me this test so I would talk about him and not myself. So I fumbled my answer.

"I'm here to work on a book," I said nervously, secretly hoping she would leave it at that. She didn't.

"What's your book about?"

Great. Now I have to say the weirdest part of all. I swallowed my pride, silently repented, and asked for the words to say:

"I'm writing a book on God's plan for us as women. How he created us and has a design for us."

She didn't seem too interested, and that was the end of it, but the experience revealed something about my own heart and this issue in our culture. Being a woman who believes that God knew what he was doing when he made us male and female is not going to move you to the top of the popular list. Following Christ never does, does it? But it does bring joy.

Our understanding of who God created us to be as women has everything to do with our display of him to a watching world. We will explore this more in chapter 1. Regardless of the flippant endorsements of feminism all around us, our task is anything but flippant. It has eternal implications for our own lives and how we reflect the image of God in this world. God had a good design for us when he created us, and our sinful hearts have been distorting that design ever since the fall.

We are not part of a rebellion against a generation gone by. We aren't thumbing our noses at the feminists of our mother's generation. Rather, we desire full-fledged restoration to what God intended for us from the very beginning. Ecclesiastes tells us that there is nothing new under the sun (1:9). Feminism, while it may seem like a new concept, is really an ideology of the oldest kind.

So I hope you will join me in the chapters ahead as I talk about what being an accidental feminist looks like. In chapter 1, we will see that God had a plan in mind when he created us as male and female, and we will begin to understand how that relates to our standing as image-bearers. The fact that you were created female matters. Chapter 2 examines the impact feminism has on our relationships with men and children, and how the Bible views our relationships with them, regardless of our marital status. Chapter 3 takes the relationship aspect further and looks at God's design for marriage. We cover heavy topics like headship and submission and why marriage is a good thing. Then we move on to our bodies and beauty in chapter 4. We will explore the usual things like purity and modesty, but we will also see that beauty and body image are not defined by our culture, men, or magazines, but by the God who made us in his image. In chapter 5 we will look at the home and why the Bible's command for a woman to be busy at home matters. This is not just a chapter for married, soon-to-be-married, or want-to-be-married women. I hope you will see how God's design for the home is one that transcends marital status. One of the common arguments regarding gender is that if a woman is gifted to lead and preach, then she should be given the opportunity to do so. Some might look down on ministries in the nursery, kitchens, and quiet corners of the church. I hope you will see in chapter 6 that the local church is a place for true human flourishing, men and women alike. Living out our true callings as men and women would not be possible without the gospel. Our ability to live as Christian women hinges on the atoning work of Christ on our behalf. In chapter 7 we consider how Christ's work is our promised hope for living according to his calling on our lives.

Each chapter provides an opportunity to apply restoration to your own life. These sections help you work through the material and make practical applications in light of your season in life. In addition each chapter includes practical examples at the end, along with study questions that can be answered with a group or on your own. My prayer is that this book would be a fruitful experience in your growth as a Christian.

I'm not making any new, innovative claims about womanhood. I'm not going to try to be hip and cool. The truth is, I don't have anything to give you other than the Word of God. And that's really all that matters at the end of the day. God's Word has a lot to say to us as women. It's clear. It's true. And it holds everything we need to know in order to live in this crazy world. I pray that we will all be more conformed to the image of Christ as we learn how he created us to be.

1

What It Means to Be a Woman

(and Not a Man)

I grew up with three younger brothers. I spent my summers at the baseball field. Football games occupied my Saturdays. Madden NFL on PlayStation was part of the family. Bodily humor eclipsed any attempted dinnertime talk about shopping, makeup, or anything civilized. It was a boy's world in the Tarter household. It was hard for Barbie to keep her girlie persona when G. I. Joe was throwing plastic bombs at her head. It was hard for me, too.

To be a girl in a house full of boys meant I had to be different. My mom made sure of that. But I often struggled. Never one to enjoy being alone, I wanted to be included, so I tried to act like my brothers. In reality, I probably just wanted a sister to play with. Either way, I did not like the differences. Thankfully, any desire I had to be "one of the boys" was short-lived. But a certain disdain for men stayed with me as I grew older.

As an adult, I liked being a woman; I just was not a big fan of men. I liked having them around when I wanted to date them or hang out with them, but I thought they were fairly useless and unhelpful in my own aspirations.

In high school and early college, I would gladly banter with any man who wanted to challenge my deeply held belief that I was just as capable, if not more, of doing everything he did. I spent a lot of energy trying to make it in a "man's world" by embracing a man's jokes, a man's understanding of sexuality, and a man's way of doing things.

Maybe you can relate. You see the opportunities the guys around you have, and you want in on the excitement. You hear disparaging comments about women, and you want to be different—or you want to show them you can be as cool as they want you to be. Or maybe you do not care. In your mind, it really makes no difference whether someone is a boy or a girl. For you, gender is little more than a difference in biology rather than a distinction inherent in one's personhood.

Or maybe you are proud of your gender. You see that God created you a female and you like it. Regardless of your understanding of what it means to be a woman, and not a man, much has happened over the last one hundred years to shape our cultural understanding of womanhood. And we might not even realize it.

Do you wonder what it means to be a woman? I mean, really wonder? Do you think it matters that God made you a female, or do you think it's simply a matter of biology? Or deep down, do you know there is a reason for the male/female distinction, but you don't know what that reason is?

If you keep your finger on the pulse of culture, it doesn't take long to find confusion about what it means to be a woman. The glossy pages and airbrushed photos of your favorite magazine tell you that being a woman means being sexy and beautiful. Television personalities tell you that being a woman means anything from having it all to being whoever you want to be.

A Question of Identity

In her 1963 book, *The Feminine Mystique,* Betty Friedan exposed the inner lives of suburban housewives. A housewife herself, Friedan noted that the women of her generation faced an identity crisis and called it the "problem that has no name."[1] Scores of women found themselves on the couches of psychiatrists wondering why, despite their stable life, happy kids, and doting husband, they couldn't seem to find fulfillment.

> The feminine mystique permits, even encourages women to ignore the question of their identity. The mystique says they can answer the question "Who am I?" by saying "Tom's wife . . . Mary's mother." But I don't think the mystique would have such power over American women if they did not fear to face this terrifying blank which makes them unable to see themselves after twenty-one. The truth is—and how long it has been true, I'm not sure, but it was true in my generation and it is true of girls growing up today—an American woman no longer has a private image to tell her who she is, or can be, or wants to be.[2]

The problem, Friedan said, was that women were finding their identity in their relationship to a husband and children, and they were coming up short. Her solution? Find your identity in yourself.

> Who knows what women can do when they are finally free to become themselves? Who knows what women's intelligence will contribute when it can be nourished without denying love? Who knows of the possibilities of love when men and women share not only children, home, and garden, not only the fulfillment of their biological roles, but the responsibilities and passions of the work that creates the human future and the full human knowledge of who they are? It has barely begun, the search of women for themselves. But the time is at hand when the voices of the feminine mystique can no longer drown out the inner voice that is driving women on to become complete.[3]

Women, Friedan said, need to define their own identity. They need to make their own future. Does that sound familiar? Friedan's legacy is alive and well today. Women now have more options than ever before. Women are no longer defined by their husband, children, or anything but their own status in society. Friedan saw the false promises of domesticity and femininity as contributing to the problem of women's identity crisis. The concept of *femininity* is rarely praised anymore (namely, the virtues of sacrifice and service to others that characterized the 1950s housewife). But are we any better for it? Or was there something to the whole "femininity" thing, even though it fell woefully short of the intended goal of giving women fulfillment and security?

Feminism's Legacy Debunked

One of the lasting impacts of feminist thought over the last one hundred years is the idea that womanhood is culturally learned, not something inherent to us as created beings. The fact that little girls want to grow up to be mothers, homemakers, or anything domestic owes only to cultural pressure, not God-given desire. The rise of the "Dad-Mom" in our cultural vernacular only seems to validate this point. With mothers now comprising a decent share of the workforce, many dads have stepped in to play the role of stay-at-home mom. It's "anything you can do I can do better" in reverse. Many assert that whether a mom stays with the kids or a dad stays with the kids has little bearing on the nature of care children receive. In the mind of the culture, men and women are interchangeable in their functions on this earth.[4]

But are they?

If you are reading this, you are most likely a woman. At some point in your life you have probably wrestled with the question, what does being female mean for me as a Christian? In this chapter, I hope to show you that being female is important and part of God's call on our lives. This chapter will lay a foundation for us as we begin our journey to restoration.

We have been fighting against God's design for a long time. Feminism continues to add to our culture's confusion regarding gender. It maintains that gender is irrelevant to the practical outworkings of our daily lives. Feminism says that yes, women are important. But besides mere biology, plumbing, and the occasional emotional outbursts, there are no differences between the sexes practically speaking. Roles are interchangeable.

Today's world embraces the idea that women are just as capable as men at doing a variety of things. Maybe you feel this way, too. The thought of limitations or differences makes you cringe. You aren't alone.

The truth is, the fact that you were created as a woman, and not a man, has practical implications for your life. But to understand what it means to be a woman in God's economy, we must first understand his design and plan for us. Then we will see that womanhood has nothing to do with our capabilities, and everything to do with what we were created for.

On one hand, some Christians say that because women, like men, are created in God's image, they have equal value and worth as an image-bearer, but they are created different by God's good design. In light of this, God has given us all different functions within his body (in the church and the home). As you probably guessed, I believe the Bible teaches this. Women like me call ourselves *complementarians*, believing that God created men and women equal, yet different. And our differences are designed to complement one another.

On the other hand, some Christians believe that being a woman created in God's image, and having equal value and worth as an image-bearer, means that our differences do not impact our function in marriage and in the body of Christ. *Giftedness* is the deciding factor, not gender. These brothers and sisters call themselves *egalitarians*. Feminism has found a home in some egalitarian circles, though not all egalitarians call themselves feminists.

So the debate rages on. Does *equality mean sameness* in roles and function, as feminism teaches? Does equality mean God frees men and women to do whatever they feel called to do? Or does equality mean something entirely different?

God's Design: The Image

Two Bible passages speak clearly about God's creation of man and woman. These passages describe life before sin entered the world. They show us God's original design for us as women. When God created the world, it was perfect in every way. Therefore, we can learn a lot about how God wants us to live just from the first few chapters of Genesis. Let's take a look at them.

> Then God said, "Let us make man in our image, after our likeness. And let them have dominion over the fish of the sea and over the birds of the heavens and over the livestock and over all the earth and over every creeping thing that creeps on the earth."
>
> So God created man in his own image,
> in the image of God he created him;
> male and female he created them. (Gen. 1:26–27)
>
> Then the LORD God said, "It is not good that the man should be alone; I will make him a helper fit for him." Now out of the ground the LORD God had formed every beast of the field and every bird of the heavens and brought them to the man to see what he would call them. And whatever the man called every living creature, that was its name. The man gave names to all livestock and to the birds of the heavens and to every beast of the field. But for Adam there was not found a helper fit for him. So the LORD God caused a deep sleep to fall upon the man, and while he slept took one of his ribs and closed up its place with flesh. And the rib that the LORD God had taken from the man he made into a woman and brought her to the man. Then the man said,
>
> "This at last is bone of my bones
> and flesh of my flesh;
> she shall be called Woman,
> because she was taken out of Man."
>
> Therefore a man shall leave his father and his mother and hold fast to his wife, and they shall become one flesh. (Gen. 2:18–24)

Genesis 1:26–27 tells us that Adam and Eve were created in God's image. One of the most fundamental things for us to learn about ourselves is that by the very nature of our being human, we are made in God's image. As a woman, you bear the image of God. Isn't that amazing? This lays the foundation for our understanding of who we are as people. To be human, and to be a woman, is to be created in the image of the God who created us.

What Is an Image?

You might be thinking, *That's great that I'm created in God's image, but what does it mean?* Good question.

When the original readers heard this, they most likely understood this to mean that man was "like God" or made to represent God. Theologian Wayne Grudem has this to say about the image of God:

> When God says, "Let us make man in our image, after our likeness" (Gen. 1:26), the meaning is that God plans to make a creature similar to himself. Both the Hebrew word for "image" (*tselem*) and the Hebrew word for "likeness" (*demut*) refer to something that is *similar* but not identical to the thing it represents or is an "image" of. The world *image* can also be used of something that *represents* something else.[5]

You and I were created to represent God on this earth. Unlike the animals, plants, and rest of creation, only Adam and Eve were given the unique stamp of bearing the image of their Creator. God called all of the rest of his creation good, but it wasn't until after he created Adam and Eve that he called his creation *very good* (see Gen. 1:31). Understanding our creation as image-bearers has implications for how we view humanity as a whole.

The Image Equals Value

The fact that you are created in the image of God means you have incredible worth and value—because God has incredible worth and value. Human beings have value because on this earth they are to represent the God who created them. God created you, made you, and loves you, and as a human being, you have been given the privilege of bearing the divine image. So when God created male and female in his image, he was telling a very important story about himself, his glory, and what he wants us to understand about him as our Creator. The fact that you were created as a woman has meaning.

This shatters the feminist notion that to emphasize the gender distinctions for women automatically makes us inferior. It can't. The biblical understanding of gender is that both genders were created in the image of God and together must have incredible worth and value. Remember how I wanted to be "one of the boys" and then morphed into a man-hater? I didn't understand this fundamental principle. As a woman created in the image of God, I have incredible worth and value. And so do the guys around me.

God's Design: Gender

So what does it all mean for us as women?

Look back at Genesis 1. Notice that God said that man (the universal term for *humankind*) was created as "male and female" in the image of God. From the beginning God had a plan. He made the man and the woman different. He gave the male certain traits and he gave the female certain traits that together adequately imaged their Creator. God could have created humanity as one androgynous creature, but he didn't. So the fact that I am a woman and my husband is a man is very important in our understanding of marriage and being created in the image of God.

This does not mean that God is either male or female, or that God has any gender. He doesn't. The creation of gender is an image of the Creator, not a point-by-point description of the Creator. So by me being female, I am imaging God in my gender. My husband is male, and he images God in his gender. Gender is important, otherwise God would not have clearly stated that he created them male and female in his image.

Before we go any further in our discussion of what it means to be a woman, we must first understand that our identity lies not in our gender but in whom our gender points to—our Creator. We find our identity in God because we bear his image. We don't find our identity in what we can do. This is where Friedan is right. She rightfully called foul on the idea that the home was the place for a woman's identity; but she swung the pendulum too far and took God out of the equation. As women, we don't find our identity in our home, our work, our body, or our marital status. We find it in the God who created us in his image. God is the Creator, and we are the created. He is the one who dictates how we are supposed to live, not the other way around. We do not get to define our identity. Rather we gain our identity in the identity of another. He has every right to tell us how he wants us to live as human beings, and specifically as women.

God's Design: The Woman

So what does it mean to be a woman? Genesis 2 tells us that after looking around at everything he had created, God saw that there was no one to complete Adam. The animals couldn't do it. The plants couldn't do it. Something was missing. So God created Eve as the suitable helper and companion for Adam. And the first marriage began.

Eve imaged God in two distinct ways: as helper and as life-giver. She was uniquely able to complete Adam as a helper in the divine calling of ruling God's creation. She was also uniquely suited to bring life into the world as "the mother of all living"—which is the meaning of her name. She possessed gifts and abilities that complemented Adam and glorified God in the garden. Life-giving is a specific and amazing quality given to women. Eve was designed to nurture, care for, and cultivate life in God's creation.

Our gender (male or female) reflects his glory. It matters that you are made female. Our humanity reflects God's glory. When we distort that and act like we are autonomous creatures, we diminish his glory. He's God! And he has all authority over our lives.

In the coming chapters we will talk more about the implications of each of these aspects of womanhood, but before we do we must first look at what God's purpose was in all of this.

God's Design: The Helper

Everything up until the middle part of Genesis 2 had been declared good. But in Genesis 2:20 and 2:28 God makes a declaration that something was not yet good in his perfect creation. The man was alone, and something was missing. Adam needed a helper. Today, this concept is often viewed as controversial or demeaning—as if a helper were someone of unequal value. But our idea of a "helper" does not necessarily line up with God's idea of a helper. The Hebrew word for helper (*ezer*) is actually used for God in other parts of the Bible: God helps his people (Ex. 18:4; Pss. 33:20; 70:5; 115:9–10).[6]

Ezer has also been used to describe God the Holy Spirit (John 14:26). How does the Holy Spirit help us? He strengthens us, he enables us to do what God has commanded us to do, he comforts us, he points us to Christ and to worship Christ, and he ministers to us by helping us better understand God's Word. There are many things that the Holy Spirit does, and not one of them is inferior to the rest of the Godhead. The Holy Spirit exists to make the Father look great and to support and strengthen the work of the Son. To be defined as a helper in these terms is in no way derogatory. It is in fact showcasing further our value as image-bearers. We image God by being a helper to our husbands. We image God by being a helper in our churches. We image God by being a helper with our roommates and coworkers. God defines himself as a helper in Scripture and allows us the opportunity to image him in this way. This is no small task.

So, what was God's intent when he called Eve the helper fit for Adam? It meant that Adam was not complete without her. Eve was created to supply strength to what was lacking in Adam's life. He needed her. As we have already seen, being created in the image of God means we are telling a story to the world about who God is. Without Eve, one crucial aspect of the triune God would be missing.

Me? A Helper?

So what does this look like for a Christian woman? In marriage, it means that God uniquely made me as a woman to help and complete what is lacking in my husband's life. It also means that being a suitable helper for a husband is unique to each marriage, not a one-size-fits-all stereotype. I must learn my husband before I can be a help to him.

One of the most important things to learn about this concept of helper in marriage is that being a suitable helper for your husband means exactly that—being a helper for *your* own husband. Every husband is different. We can't look at another couple and compare relationships. It is like comparing apples to oranges. The same goes for our abilities. It is impossible to compare our lives and how we serve others to those around us, namely because we are all created differently with unique abilities given to us by God.

When my husband and I were first married, I struggled with this concept. In my mind, I thought being his helper was whatever I defined it to be. I was okay at making sure dinner was on the table, making his lunch, and doing the laundry. But when it came time for him to write a paper, and he wanted me to talk through his points with him, I feigned interest and often became frustrated that he was interrupting what I wanted to be doing in that moment. It bothered me. It was getting in the way of my time to myself. And then it hit me (though not fast enough): God made my husband a verbal processer and gave me an interest in theological things. My husband needs to talk to process his thoughts, and I like to talk about those very things. Now that he is a lay pastor and preaches a number of times a year, he still asks me to help him talk through a passage of Scripture as he is preparing to preach. This is unique to both of us, but I think that's what God had in mind when he made Eve a suitable helper for Adam. He created Adam and he created Eve, and with each of their strengths and weaknesses they complemented one another.

But what if you aren't married and marriage is not in your immediate future? You can still be a helper. The qualities inherent to being a suitable helper are qualities that can be exhibited in your life even now as you seek to encourage, strengthen, comfort, and support those who are in your life. All who work have some authority over them. Learn your boss; ask God to show you ways you can be most helpful in your work for him or her. Grow in your observation of others. At the end of a long day of work is your roommate overwhelmed by making dinner for herself? Offer to help her or listen to her difficulties at her job. Can you think of a creative way to meet a need in your local church that works with your particular gifting? All of these are ways you can grow in being a helper who serves and supports those who are in authority over you. Growing as a helper means having a Philippians 2:5–11 mindset, where we consider humility and service as more important than our own immediate glory. It is not demeaning, any more than Christ laying his life down for us was demeaning of his full deity. God gets glory and others see his beauty.

God presents himself as a helper in Scripture and allows us the opportunity to image him in this way. So the best way to grow in womanhood right now is not to master Proverbs 31, but to grow in godliness and love for Christ. As you grow in your knowledge of your Creator, fight sin in your life, and study his Word, imaging God with a servant's heart will be a whole lot easier.

In my life, my problem was that I was trying to master a stereotype rather than trying to love my husband. I was trying to fit into a box of my own making, not seeking to serve the husband God had given me. Helping my husband looks different from how my friend might help her husband, but that is how God designed it to be. It is not one-size-fits-all. That would be terribly boring, wouldn't it? I'm called to develop and implement my giftedness for the good of my husband, so God gets glory.

God's Design: The Life-Giver

In addition to being a helper, Eve was uniquely designed to image God in another way. While Adam and Eve were both given the command to be fruitful and multiply, Eve bore the unique task of bearing life. Adam named her Eve, because she was the mother of all living (Gen. 3:20). Her name literally means "life-giver." It gets to the core of what it means to be a woman created in God's image.

Perhaps the most obvious way Eve exercised dominion over the creation and showed forth her God-given image-bearing qualities was by carrying and nurturing life—from the earliest stages of pregnancy to the fostering of life in her own home with her husband and children.

Note that when Adam named his wife Eve, she had not yet given birth to a child. Yet she was still called the "mother of all living." This has tremendous implications for you, whether you are a physical mother or not. Susan Hunt explains:

> Mothers give life, not just birth. Every woman is called to be a life-giver in every relationship and ministry God entrusts to our care. All redeemed women are mothers in Israel. Words of encouragement give life to the discouraged. Ministries of compassion infuse life into the weary and worn. Ministries of availability and hospitality beyond kith and kin model the covenant way of life. Ministries to unsaved neighbors give glimpses of life. When we live the life of *hesed* [lovingkindness], we impart life in myriad mothering roles.[7]

Me? A Life-Giver?

Maybe you are in the middle of your junior year of high school or graduating from college. You think, *How can I be a life-giver? I can't have kids yet. I'm so busy. I don't even know what to do around babies.*

This is why Hunt's definition is so helpful. There is a plethora of "mothering" opportunities that don't require you to end up on the latest MTV show about teenage pregnancy. The coming chapters will spark your creativity when thinking through how this applies to your life. But here let me give you a couple of examples.

Andrea is a single woman who loves Jesus. In fact, she loves

Jesus so much that she lives in the inner city of Minneapolis so she can minister to the people there. Her jobs have changed throughout the years, but her commitment to the people of her neighborhood hasn't. From running with her neighbor to hosting a cooking class for neighborhood kids to tutoring at the nearby school, she, along with others from her church, has made this little neighborhood her mission field. She is providing the hope of Christ to many kids who have very little stability and little to no Christian influence. She is using her womanhood to nurture and cultivate life in kids who desperately need it. She is a life-giver.

My friend, Katie, is also using her singleness to be a life-giver. Instead of spending her single years enjoying her free time and pursuing her own interests, she has been involved in a variety of ministries over the years, from leading women's Bible studies to volunteering at a crisis pregnancy center. She believes that her single years are not to be wasted and that God has uniquely created her to serve him in this season, however long it may be. And she embodies what it means to be a life-giver not just in her church and in other obvious "ministry places." Katie sees her coworkers as image-bearers in need of Christ. Instead of using her workplace as a means to her own glory, she works hard, models what it means to follow Christ, and shares the gospel with those who will listen. When she works hard and is different from others around her, people take notice. This is life giving. This is living out the image of God as a woman in a particular season of life.

This is God's design for us as women, to grow as helpers and life-givers so that he gets the glory and we are fulfilled. But a quick look around tells us that something is not right here. If everything was how God intended it to be, we would not need to recover from anything, would we?

God's Design Distorted

We don't have to look very far in Genesis to see that something terrible happened. Genesis 3 paints a devastating picture of the fall of mankind. This has tremendous relevance for us as we understand God's purpose in creation. Satan tempted and brought down humanity by getting at the heart of who God created us to be—male and female.

Notice that Satan went to the woman rather than to the man. Some have argued that this implies that the woman was more gullible or naive than the man. But that would contradict their equality as human beings. Satan knew God's design for marriage and gender. He knew that God placed Adam in the garden as the leader of his family. He knew that Adam was supposed to be the protector of Eve and all of God's creation. He knew that Eve was to follow Adam and help him fulfill his role in the garden. So Satan blatantly challenged God's good design by saying these fateful words:

"Did God actually say?" (Gen. 3:1).

So much hinges on Eve's response to this question. Can God be trusted? Can God's design and purpose for you be the most fulfilling thing in your life? Is God's word really that important and authoritative? Satan hated the image of God inherent in the man and woman's created order. This is still true today. He will stop at nothing to destroy what our image-bearing represents—our great God, the saving work of his Son, Jesus, and the indwelling presence of his Spirit. Satan hates God, and he hates us representing God on this earth. It's no wonder that so much of our sin, temptation, and problems are directly related to who we are as image-bearers.

We all know what happened. Eve believed the lie and ate the fruit, and her husband followed suit. Adam was right there with Eve, and he ate along with her. When sin entered the world, so did strife between the sexes. Men and women have been in a battle for control ever since. As we have already seen, feminism at its core is a challenge to authority, and ultimately God's authority. Adam and Eve wanted to be God. They did not believe that his word to them was true. They did not believe that he had ultimate authority over their lives. And now here we are.

Consequences Are Gender Specific

Women often joke about the curse brought on us by Eve. When we talk about childbirth, we blame Eve for the pain we experience. When our monthly cycle comes around, we lightheartedly say it's all Eve's fault. But the curse that God gave in the garden is actually far more serious than physical pain. In addition to the most devastating judgment, spiritual and physical death, the curse on the man and woman hit at the heart of who they were as male and female. No longer would the design be very good. No longer would God's glory be perfectly displayed in his image-bearing creatures. Being a man or a woman would now be marked with suffering, strife, and pain.

To show how important gender is to God, he cursed them at the core of who they were as man and woman. For the man, the curse targeted his role as provider and protector (Gen. 3:17–19). Adam failed to lead, protect, and provide for God's creation by failing to guard and keep both the garden that God created and the wife that God had given as a helper to him. He allowed Satan (an enemy of God) to tempt his wife, and he listened to his wife rather than standing up to her and for her. When God confronted them about their sin, God calls to Adam, not Eve. Although Eve is the one who was tempted and ate first, God holds Adam responsible for his failure of leadership. As a result, life for Adam would be more difficult, specifically in his work. Caring for God's creation would be hard. The ground wouldn't bear life like it once did, and the man would have to work harder to provide. The most physically draining day on the job or monotonous day staring at your computer screen is a reminder that work is cursed.

The creation would now also be cursed, making Adam's task of protecting his family much harder. This carries over to today. Murder happens. Bad things happen to families all of the time. Death is imminent. God's creation is now groaning for redemption (Rom. 8:22).

Being a protector would also be harder because now man's sinful nature would want to flee from such responsibility. Before the fall, Adam would have desired to protect, provide for, and lead his family. Now that desire will be the opposite. It will be a fight to desire rightly.

We see this all around us today. Just a few years ago, a cruise ship crashed off the coast of Italy. While it is a universal understanding that the captain always stays with his ship to ensure the protection of everyone on board, this captain fled the ship while innocent people died. At the time of this writing, he was on trial because of his cowardice and manslaughter. While we see glimpses of God's original design and intent for men to lead, provide, and protect, we see the devastation of the fall all around us with men fleeing their responsibilities, like Adam did, on a regular basis. The passivity and apathy toward leading, protecting, and providing for God's creation (the earth, family, wife, sphere of influence) began with Adam and curses us to this day. It is not how God intended it to be.

A New Woman Emerges

In the aftermath of sin's crushing arrival in this world, a new woman emerged from the rubble. Eve too was cursed specifically, most notably in two distinct ways—pain in childbearing and strife in the marital relationship (Gen. 3:16).

In the coming chapters we will look in greater detail at how Christ crushes the curse, but it is important for us to gain a solid foundation before we get into any practical application of womanhood.

Eve was created to bring life into this world, but what was intended to be the greatest joy would now be laced with the greatest pain. She would have pain in childbearing. This strikes at the heart of her distinctiveness as the mother of all living. Of course she would now face physical pain in the actual delivery of children, but she would also face pain in other areas. Infertility. Loss of children through miscarriage, stillbirth, or the death of a child. Children who throw temper tantrums. Wayward children. Children who reject their Creator. The bond that a mother feels with her child now is often the source of her greatest suffering.

Embedded within this curse is another devastating reality. The marriage relationship would now be marked by strife, not bliss.

Genesis 3:16 gives the judgment, "Your desire shall be for your husband, and he shall rule over you." The interpretation of this verse is much debated among complementarians and egalitarians. The word for *desire* is the same word used in the story of Cain and Abel, when God tells Cain that sin's *desire* is for him, meaning that sin wants to overtake him (Gen. 4:7). God tells Cain that he "must rule over it"—or master it. In the curse in the garden, God tells Eve that her desire would now be to overrule her husband, to take over his leadership, to dominate him, and to control him. And what happens in return? The man will try to "rule over" her. There will now be an ongoing struggle between the man and the woman for leadership in the marriage relationship. God's original design of perfect unity in marriage by loving leadership and willing submission (more on that later) is now distorted.

We see this tension played out in a variety of ways: nagging, controlling, constant criticizing, undermining a husband's authority through dominance or passive aggressive behavior. The wife no longer delights in submitting to and respecting her husband. It is a struggle and a constant fight to live within God's design.

Since the fall, women have been in a battle not only against our own flesh and sin, but also against the men in our lives. You might not be married, but you most certainly relate to men in some capacity. Do you respect them? Do you treat them as fellow image-bearers or as useless individuals? Do you use men to get what you want? Or do you feel like you have to be like them to get anywhere in this world? Do you engage in "boy bashing" sessions with your girlfriends? This is the heart of feminism in action.

What Is the Point?

That was a lot to take in, wasn't it? Maybe you read the stuff about marriage and childbearing and think, *That is way far away from my world right now. What does it matter for me now?*

If that's you, you are asking good questions. The fact that you were created as a woman—and not a man—has tremendous implications for how you live in this world. It matters. Your gender is not some arbitrary construct of your upbringing, culture, or even your own desires. It is part of who you are. You might not be married, but you were created to be a helper and life-giver by the sheer fact that God created you as a female. He is our Creator, and he tells us how we are supposed to live. But there is something even more important to understand about womanhood before we move on.

Womanhood is about God. You were created as a woman to image God to a watching world. When you deny that, or treat it as irrelevant, you are not reflecting the glory of your Creator like you were designed to do. This has tremendous implications for your life. It matters if you renounce marriage and children for a career. It matters if you have boy-bashing parties with your friends after a bad breakup. It matters if you dress immodestly or make out with guys just for fun. It matters if you submit to your husband. It matters if you want to preach in your church on a Sunday morning. These actions tell a story not only about you, but about the God who made you. The very fact that you were created in God's image has implications for how you live the rest of your life.

Restoration in My Life

In order to recover from feminism and our rebellion against God's design, we must understand what he expects of us. Here are some examples for how to grow in restoration in your own life. The list is not exhaustive, and you should not feel like you have to do all of these things in order to be godly. In the coming chapters, I will more specifically address women in varying seasons. For now, here are some ideas for women in every stage of life. Recovering from feminism and embracing womanhood should come out of who you are, and should not be forced on you.

First, and foremost, grow as a Christian. If you are not a Christian, read the last chapter to learn more about this Christ who came to save people from their sin. He is your only hope for truly living out your design as a woman. If you are a Christian, invest in your spiritual growth through study of Scripture, faithful church involvement, and prayer. Being a godly woman is a fruit of a changed life, and it is only when you grow as a Christian that fruit begins to blossom in your life. Since you are created in God's image, womanhood begins with knowing and loving the God who created you.

Second, grow in who you are as a woman. "Helper" and "life-giver" are not individual personality traits. They are to be part of who you are. These aspects of womanhood look different for every woman. Learn what it means to serve, to die to your desires and wants, and to ask God to make you more like his Son, Jesus. Cultivate life in the people around you through service, Bible studies, or mentoring relationships. Work with children, or explore how you can serve others through your job. The opportunities are endless. The best place to experience growth is in the context of your local church, which we will talk about in chapter 6.

Third, learn where you are gifted and cultivate those gifts. Your local church is also the best place to find out where you are gifted. When I was single, I poured my life into my local church, serving in the nursery and with youth, and attending women's events. I sought out older women to model service for me. You have unique gifts and abilities that were specifically given to you by God, and the best place to learn what they are is in your local church.

Study Questions

1. Confusion about what it means to be a woman in our fallen world abounds. We all struggle with God's design for us in some way. How do you specifically struggle with God's design for women? How does the Bible provide hope for that struggle?

2. What does it mean to be equal in value and worth, yet different in function?

3. Where might you live out your calling as a life-giver or helper, married or not?

4. What are some ways that women uniquely image God?

2

What Women Want

"You know what women really want?" a friend emphatically asked after telling me about her recent break-up.

"They just want the man to make the decision. They don't want to have to decide where to eat when they are hungry. I mean, I'm a feminist, but I want him to just make a decision sometimes."

My friend had been lamenting the ups and downs of her relationship that spanned a number of years, and what it all came down to was this: she just wanted the man to make an effort. Even with something as simple as choosing where to eat. Her boyfriend was fairly certain that he wanted to marry her after all these years, but when it came to the little, daily decisions, he just wasn't cutting it for her. She wanted more decisiveness. And so she broke up with him.

My friend's story was interesting to me because she wasn't well-versed in the rhetoric of Christianity or our notions of womanhood. In fact, she was (and still is) a self-proclaimed agnostic and feminist who didn't feel like she needed a man or the gospel. She didn't care if she measured up to the Proverbs 31 woman or the models set forth in Scripture. I doubt she even knew that God cared about the differences between men and women. So while her lament about her ex-boyfriend's inability to choose an appropriate dining option might seem unreasonable, I think she was on to something. That a twenty-something feminist would make such a pronounced statement about her own relational desires and the conflicting nature of them reveals something about how God created us to be.

My friend was making a statement, albeit a cloudy one, about men and women. For all the talk about women advancing, defining themselves, and being on the same playing field as men, for the most part women still expect something from the men in their lives. That expectation is rooted in our differences as male and female. As we saw in chapter 1, God created men and women differently. He created them equal in his image, but he gave them different roles to play for his glory. All people, because they bear God's image, can see or feel (whether they realize it or not) that there is something uniquely different about men and women. And this has a bearing on what we desire and how we relate to each other.

What Women Want

As women, we have an innate desire to be led and provided for. Actress Kirsten Dunst said in an April 2014 interview that "sometimes, you need your knight in shining armor. You need a man to be a man and a woman to be a woman. That's why relationships work."[1] But as a result of the fall and the influence of feminism, women often deny that they want a "man to be a man." We experience a tension—we want men to provide and protect when it is helpful to us, but at the same time we want our freedom and independence. My friend, for all her critiques of her boyfriend's lack of decision making skills, also wanted her own space. Much of the time she couldn't decide *what* she wanted.

When the first wave of the feminist movement burst on the scene, it radicalized how women related to men. Prior to the suffragist movement of the late nineteenth and early twentieth centuries, women were defined by their relationship to a man, primarily their husbands or fathers. Slowly, this definition started to change and women became more independent. Today, women are defined by nothing other than their very selves. As we've noted, this development is not all bad. Women gained the ability to own property, make financial decisions, and vote. These are all good changes. But the budding independence of first-wave feminism lead to the confusion we see today when it comes to romantic relationships between the sexes. Women can't seem to escape their God-given desire for companionship, protection, and self-sacrificing love from a man—yet many are haunted by a little voice in their heads telling them they can and should make it on their own.

Social critic Kay Hymowitz wrote an indicting book in 2011 called *Manning Up: How the Rise of Women Has Turned Men into Boys*. Based on her research, what women want is puzzling at best and downright selfish at worst. Women, Hymowitz says, want the best of both worlds. They want the chivalry of yesteryear coupled with the lack of restraint afforded to women today. Women want freedom, and they want family. They want to be independent of a man, and they want to be with one all the same. But it's not your grandmother's world anymore. Gone are the days of *Mad Men*-era expectations of women. Women hold the cards and make the rules now, but this has caused an even bigger problem, Hymowitz finds. True men are evaporating quicker than water on a hot summer's day. What is left is what she calls the "child-man"—and his attempts at chivalry are virtually nonexistent.[2] When women act like men, she observes, men wither away.

Nowhere is this tension more evident than in the dating relationship (as my friend found to be true). Hymowitz writes:

> The dinner check quandary captures the puzzling predicament of young men in pursuit: they are caught between women's persistent attraction to male vigor, or manhood of an old-fashioned variety, and the vibrator-powered womanhood of today. On the one hand, a woman wants Ashley Wilkes, all sensitivity and soulfulness and attention to "her needs." On the other, she wants Rhett Butler, sultry, confident, and capable of the grand gesture. If on Valentine's Day he gives her a single stem, she may

> be all "One rose? That's it?" If he wants to get married, he has to plan a proposal on the order of a Hollywood production. If men and women are equals, it makes no sense to expect men to propose. Shouldn't a couple make a decision together, as they would about where to go for brunch?[3]

Hymowitz sees the dilemma. Do you? If you are like me, you have probably experienced this very tension at some point in your life, or at least heard your girlfriends lamenting it. A guy can't seem to win for trying, yet a girl can't seem to figure out what she really wants.

Women want men to treat them with the chivalry and respect of a generation gone by, but they don't want it too much . . . that would just be weird. And a little insulting, right? Hymowitz goes on to say, "Everyone knows the woman who calls herself a feminist but still wants 'a guy to be a guy' or something along the lines of 'I didn't need a guy to take care of me, but I wouldn't want to be with someone who couldn't.'"[4]

Feminism has changed the way women relate to men. It took women from a place of dependence to independence. But as Hymowitz notes, feminism has also confused women in their attempts at relating to men. Now that women don't need a man, men are on their way to becoming obsolete and useless. And that's not good for anyone.

Relating to Men as Christian Women

Of course, not every woman feels that men are on their way to extinction. Even if you might not consider yourself a strong feminist, Christian women often face this same tension. You and I are "in the world" in every literal sense of the phrase. We own property. We vote. We have jobs that provide us amazing opportunities for advancement and flourishing. We date. We marry. We have children. But we are called to not be "of the world" (John 15:9; Rom. 12:2). We feel the tension when we bristle at the man who tries to help us, yet deep down we want him to cherish us. We want to hold onto our freedom, but we don't want chivalry to be dead.

Maybe you think you don't struggle with this tension as much as other women. But have you ever spent a night in your apartment lamenting the failed romantic attempts of the last guy you dated? You might not scoff at the guy who holds the door for you, but those late-night boy-bashing sessions aren't much better. You might not want to revolt against the chivalry of men around you, but disdain and gossip reveal the very same tension. We want men around, but only on our terms. We want them, but we have little grace for when they fail us.

I think the Bible provides us with another way of relating to men, other than scoffing at their chivalry or expecting them to be Mr. Darcy.

As Christian women, we have a unique and wonderful opportunity to be an encouragement to the men in our lives. Unlike my friend's frustrated remarks, and subsequent termination of her relationship, we can use our words and desires to spur our Christian brothers on to be the kind of men God made us to yearn for, and the kind of men that he made them to be.

As I reflected on my conversation with my friend, three particular applications for encouragement came to mind:

1. You can encourage the men in your life when they do lead, exhibit godly character, or pursue a woman.
2. You can be patient when they don't lead in this way—or are slower than we would like.
3. You can be willing to ask the men in your life for help.

Molly works for a Christian nonprofit as a marketing manager. In her line of work it is easy to focus solely on the tasks at hand. And there are many. There are always projects to complete, newsletters to write, print campaigns to launch, and emails to answer. But her boss doesn't start with the to-do list in their weekly meetings. Instead, he starts with prayer and a brief word from Scripture.

Initially, Molly was anxious by this use of precious time. She is task-oriented, and this was not a task she saw as necessary to their main objectives. But over time she has grown to see that the slower start to their Monday meetings actually calms her nerves and reorients her priorities in a good way. So she tells her boss that she appreciates his leadership in this way. Knowing her personality, her boss is encouraged to see that his effort to provide spiritual leadership for his employees is not in vain.

Sarah has been trying to help her brother find a girlfriend, like all good big sisters do. James has had a string of disappointing relationships, and he is fearful about moving forward with another one. But he has been enjoying his time with a woman from church and would like to ask her out for coffee. Because of his fear of another failed relationship, James is hesitant. Over time he finds the courage to ask this woman out, hoping for the best. Before the date, Sarah encourages James in his pursuit of this relationship. Even with the prospect of rejection that comes with all relationships, she shows him that his step forward is actually God's kind work in his life to trust God for the outcome. She doesn't linger on his slowness to initially act, but instead points to how God is working in his life.

Carrie teaches a children's Sunday school class at her church. In recent months she has noticed the boys in her class growing unruly. Carrie's friend Sam is really good with young children and has taught this class before, so she decides to enlist him for help. Instead of trying to tackle the problem on her own, she seeks Sam's help with her classroom, and by doing so encourages him in his leadership gifts.

So how do you encourage the men in your life? Do you ask for help when you need it, or do you try to tackle everything on your own? Do you have a friend who mentors an at-risk youth, like a guy I know? Acknowledge that. What about the guys in your small group who get up every morning and work faithfully at their jobs? That is no small task; find ways to thank them for that. C. J. Mahaney calls this pointing out "evidences of grace" in the lives of other believers.[5] You can encourage men whether you are single or married. If you are single, it can mean thanking a Christian brother for planning group activities or leading a church Bible study. The most practical thing you can do is to make words of encouragement a part of your daily vocabulary. (This obviously also applies to those in a relationship.) Ephesians 4:29 talks about using our words to "build others up." Proverbs 16:24 says that sweet words bring health to the body; they are life giving. It is easy to tear down with our words, but noticing God's grace in a person's life takes work and a good dose of grace on our part. Ask God to show you evidences of grace in the lives of the men around you and testify to that grace by acknowledging what you've seen. If you are in a relationship with a Christian brother, you can encourage him as he works at leading you. In my experience, I've seen that encouragement can be the fuel to continue leading well.

This practice of encouragement will serve you as you prepare for marriage, if that is what God has planned for you. Married women have the opportunity to encourage their husbands daily. It is far easier to see your husband's flaws, so the practice of encouragement will take some discipline. This is an area of my own life where I fall woefully short. But in the moments where God has given me the grace to encourage my husband, rather than tear him down or be quick to criticize, I have seen God work tremendously to grow us and our marriage (Prov. 15:1–2). One thing I have found to be particularly helpful is reminding myself that when I have been the target of criticism, I fall into the pit of despair. I don't want to do that very thing to my husband. It is important to remember what Christ has done on my husband's behalf. One practical thing I have tried to do is thank God for the evidences of grace I see in his life. It's hard to endlessly criticize when I am reminding myself of the ways God has worked in making him more like himself.

We must understand that the men in our lives will fail us, sometimes terribly. Whether it is a father, brother, friend, pastor, or husband, at some point we will be disappointed, and even heartbroken, by a man's lack of Christlikeness. But the reality is, we will often disappoint them as well. We will never treat one another rightly all of the time. This is why we need Christ all of the time. We need a daily, strong dose of remembering Christ's work to enable us to live as God's image-bearers.

If we are going to make any progress in bearing with the failings of the men in our lives, we are going to need patience (Matt. 18:21–22; 1 Thess. 5:14). And I imagine they will need the same with us. Patience is not my specialty. What I've realized is that often my lack of patience stems from unmet unrealistic expectations. If a brother in Christ is slow to ask a girl out, perhaps patience would be the remedy for his lack of action. If your boyfriend doesn't understand that you want him to make a particular decision, perhaps communicating what you want in a humble and kind manner would help him. Paul says in Philippians 1:6 that "he who began a good work in you will bring it to completion at the day of Jesus Christ." We are to be patient with men because we trust that the God who saved them will bring them all the way home to that final day with Jesus (Phil. 1:6).

In all of these things, it is important to never condone unrepentant, continual sin. But it is important to extend grace to our brothers, as we would like them to extend grace to us. I heard a pastor once say that all we get from Jesus is grace. He doesn't give us the silent treatment. He doesn't see us as lost causes when we sin. He doesn't lash out in a hateful tone when we don't do what he commands. He convicts us of sin and provides a way for us to sin no more.

Male/female relationships are hard. If they were easy, we wouldn't need to depend on God for his supernatural grace. My friend was right: women want men to be decision-makers. We were made to follow a man. But more importantly, we were made to follow the God-man—Jesus. He is our ultimate head and leader. And he is our hope when all else fails us. Instead of banking all our hope on a fallen man, let us instead put all our hope in Christ.

It will change our attitudes toward the sinners we are in relationships with, and it will conform us more into Christ's image.

Women and Children

Feminism didn't just change the way we relate to men. Though in the past women were predominately defined by their relationship with a man, they were also defined by their roles as mothers. As recently as sixty years ago, most women could expect to marry and have children at a relatively young age. Now, however, most women do not marry until their mid- to late twenties, and many don't even think about children until thirty or after. To be fair, not all women are marrying or having children later by choice. But that's a topic for another time. Here I don't intend to focus on the age of marriage and having children, but on changes in our cultural attitude toward children.

Ask any graduating college senior if she plans on having a baby anytime soon and she will most likely give you a blank stare. Feminism gave women options, and with those options came the ability to "control" your fertility. Or, at least, seemingly control it.

Gone are the days of college coeds dreaming of a husband, children, and a white picket fence. The pendulum has swung. In many ways, our culture now views children as an obstacle to true happiness and success. Babies change your life and your body. Why waste your most productive years on a little person who can't give you anything in return?

But God has another idea. One of the first commandments he gave to Adam and Eve was to "be fruitful and multiply" (Gen. 1:28). God values children, and he values the family. He calls children a blessing (Ps. 127:3). When Christ was on the earth, he regularly ministered to children, even rebuking his disciples for trying to drive them away (Matt. 19:14; Luke 18:16). Even his disciples thought children were a hindrance to real ministry and a fruitful life. But God loves children. He wants people to have them and to appreciate them. In fact, God even refers to Christians as his children, confirming the fact that God holds children in high regard (1 John 3:1).

So what does this mean for you? It means that motherhood is a good and wise thing. The very fact that you were created as female means that you were designed to be a mother. As we saw in chapter 1, when Adam named his wife the "life-giver," he was making a profound statement about her glorious function in God's economy. From her, life would come. From her, the lineage of Adam would continue. From her, the Christ would come and make all things right. As women, we are given the great opportunity to bring life into the world. We are commissioned to care for the next generation through our daily sacrifice of caring for, training, and raising our children. And not just our children, but any children God puts in our path. This means that single and married women alike can embrace God's delight in children. I know that having children is not an option for many women. The second half of this chapter will address this reality.

Of course, our identity as Christian women should never be in what we can do, produce, or accomplish. This applies to motherhood as well. But that doesn't mean God didn't have a purpose in creating us as beings who by our very nature can bear life.

Every few months, it seems that another celebrity or leader comes out sharing why she chose to never have children. Usually the statement is something akin to "I was too selfish to have children" or "I knew I wanted a career more than children." I am thankful these women have the courage to be this honest. They are simply saying what other women are probably thinking but don't have the platform or guts to say publicly. But this sort of response is a sad commentary on the state of our current culture. As a Christian, you have the amazing opportunity to live in a different way—not so you can get glory or be awarded "Mom of the Year." But rather so God gets the glory by your faithful life. You can speak the truth about how God created you to be as a woman through your joy in this task of life-giving. Whether through your profession as a teacher, your service to your church, your investment in your friends and neighbors, or your daily labors as a momma to kids who depend on you—you are a life-giver and are showing with your life that children have value. Remember my friend Andrea from chapter 1? She daily puts to death the cultural disdain for children. Her intentional pursuit of the families in her neighborhood tells a beautiful story about God's good design for women to be life-givers.

Calling Us Blessed

The Proverbs 31 woman is a much-debated character in Scripture. Many women spend their lives trying to live up to her example, yet find themselves falling painfully short (myself included). Because she sets such a high bar, many women find it easiest to dismiss her, but there is much to be learned by her life. Every culture show disregard for children to some degree, and the ancient Near East was no different. A quick survey of the Old Testament reveals that the Israelites were markedly different in their approach to children (or at least they were to supposed to be). While the nations around them were sacrificing children to idols, Israel was to hold children in high regard—because God himself did. The Proverbs 31 woman did not see them as trash to be discarded or a hindrance to her plans. She cared for them. In verse 28, we read that the fruit of her labors as a life-giving mother to her children is that they rose up and called her blessed. This is the result of a life lived for the good of one's children

One cold January day in 2011, my husband and I attended the funeral of his dear grandmother. Her mind had long deteriorated by the time I met her shortly after our wedding. I never knew her in her "glory days," which my husband likes to recall. But from what I've heard from the four living children and many grandchildren she left behind, she was a remarkable lady. She was in her late eighties when she died and had outlived two beloved husbands. In her long life she birthed five children who lived (one set of twins) and had numerous grandchildren and great-grandchildren. Every holiday she gladly hosted her family at her farm and made them feel welcome. I heard countless stories of eating peaches on a hot summer day, playing football in her yard, and playing games at her kitchen table. Her family most certainly rose up and called her blessed. When she died, the loss was felt deeply.

But the Proverbs 31 woman is not just an example for married women. Consider Amy Carmichael. She gave up the comfort of her life in Ireland to be a missionary to India. Through her faithful, courageous service many children were rescued from temple prostitution and brought to the refuge of the Dohnavur Fellowship. In a culture that viewed children as pawns in their religious idolatry, Amy showed them something different. She valued the children. She believed their lives mattered. She educated them. She told them of Christ. As a result, many came to trust in the very Christ she loved and gave her life for.

It can be easy for some to place little value on children. They can't do much of anything for themselves. They do change your life in profound (and sometimes difficult) ways. But as Christians, we know that this life is not all there is. As Christian women, we are uniquely given the great opportunity to train the next generation to love God, his Word, and his people.

What about Me Now?

One of the biggest critiques of God's design for women is that it fails to take into account the single or childless woman. Critics say it presents a cookie-cutter model of womanhood that only the married mother of four can fit into. Point taken.

You might be wondering how all of this applies to the single and childless women today. Perhaps reading about the blessing of children or the purpose of marriage is painful for you. You would love to be holding a baby in your arms. You would love to be learning how to relate to a man who loves you and wants to be with you. You find yourself asking, Did God make a mistake with me? If having children and being a godly wife are part of God's good plan for women, am I missing the mark somehow?

I can relate.

While getting married at twenty-six is hardly old by today's standards, until then I often felt like I was waiting for my life to begin. I graduated from college, watched two of my younger brothers get married, and started a career on my own. In the years since my feminist days, I had slowly started to value the ideas of marriage and children. Even if I wasn't ready to admit it, deep down I felt the pull toward marriage and children. As I grew as a believer and got involved in my local church, I saw godly families with happy moms and dads and thriving children. What I once saw as a mild form of lifelong bondage, I now saw as appealing. But marriage and children didn't happen in the timetable I planned. I wanted to put all of the biblical things I had been learning into practice, yet I had no man and no children. Fast forward a few years, and I found myself in a similar situation when I lost our first child through miscarriage and faced two years of painful infertility after the loss. Again, my plan for my life was not happening like I thought it would. Was this whole godly woman thing for me?

Any discussion of God's plan for women as they relate to men and children must carry with it a fair amount of realism. Not every woman is a wife, nor is she a mother. Some deeply desire marriage and children and are regularly slapped in the face with harsh disappointment.

So how do you relate to men and children when you are in what feels like womanhood purgatory? First, acknowledge that it's not purgatory. You aren't in a special category of misfits. You aren't an outsider looking in on the kingdom of God. Your womanhood is not reduced to your biological function or a marriage license.

When sin entered the world, everything was distorted. As we saw in the first few chapters of Genesis, we are given part of God's plan for humanity—be fruitful and multiply. But within a few short chapters, we find barrenness and strife among the sexes

(Genesis 11). Sin has devastating consequences. Now, don't hear me saying that your singleness or childlessness is the result of your own personal sin. While I don't know your story, I can say that it probably is not. But the presence of sin and the curse that is upon everything has infected every facet of our world—including our relationships and our ability to bear life.

The harsh reality is that in this fallen world, Genesis 1–2 cannot be fully realized. Sure, we are given glimmers of hope throughout the darkness. Many women get married young, have happy marriages, and have children without any problem. Praise God for that. But for every success story there is an alternative story lurking in the shadows. God's design for women is most certainly for the women in those stories, too.

The principles of learning how to relate to the men in your life are not intended only for marriage. Being a godly woman is more about a heart that trusts in God than it is about a list of rules you must follow. In 1 Peter, Sarah is praised ultimately because she hoped in God, not because she submitted to her husband (1 Pet. 3:5–6). She obeyed Abraham because she trusted in the God who was holding her circumstances together. She is praised for her faith, and her submission was the outworking of that faith. As you grow in godliness, and if you deeply desire marriage, know that your daily labor to trust the God who has not forgotten you is doing far more for your growth as a woman than you realize. God's design is for all women because it is about the God who made us, not about our position in life. It is about trusting in the One who created us and holds our future in his hands. We cannot assume marriage and motherhood for all women.

The same is true for those who are married, yet long for children. You might look at your life and feel incomplete. The very thing you were created to do doesn't seem to be happening for you. Maybe you feel like a failure. Maybe you feel like a broken vessel. Maybe you feel like you have no value in God's kingdom. Oh dear sister, you do. By virtue of being a woman, you bear the ability to be a life-giver. Of course, this looks different for you right now. And it might carry the sting of being unable to bear life the way you so desperately long to, but you have the ability nonetheless. Adam named his wife "the mother of all living" *before* she bore him any children. Her identity as a life-giver was rooted in her creation as a woman, not in her function as a baby maker. Susan Hunt says it this way:

> We tend to have a myopic view of mothering. We limit it to women who have birthed biologically. The covenant way is bigger and bolder. Every redeemed woman is a life-giver. Failure to understand this biblical perspective diminishes motherhood. The results:
>
> We will be shortsighted and fail to extend our life-giving capacity into every single relationship.
>
> Single and barren women are deprived of the joy of fulfilling their creational life-giving design, and the covenant community is denied their mothering ministry.[6]

So while we cannot assume marriage and motherhood for all women, God's good design is for every woman, even those who might currently feel like less of a woman. I promise you, in Christ, you are as complete of a woman as the wife and mother standing next to you. Maybe some of you are called to the single life. God has given you a ministry, purpose, or mission field that requires a single-minded focus, much like Amy Carmichael. These principles apply to you as well. Like Amy, you can value children and even marriage as you live as a single woman.

The "It Can Wait" Phenomenon

Maybe you are reading this and thinking, *I'm not infertile. I just don't want kids yet,* or, *I want to get married, I just want to wait until I get settled first.* Many circumstances require delaying marriage and having children. Perhaps you are waiting to go on the mission field. Perhaps your husband is preparing to enter medical school, and adding a child would not be financially wise at this time. Or maybe your parents are dead-set against you getting married while you are in college and there is no swaying them. Again, these are valuable reasons to consider waiting. But I want to challenge you a bit on this. Obviously, there is no law in Scripture that says you *must* get married and have children immediately. But for a moment I want to speak not to the woman who desperately wants these things in her life right now, but to the one who thinks they can wait.

Can they? Or better yet, should they?

Kay Hymowitz sees a growing trend among young people:

> Under the circumstances, one thing the young grad is not going to plan is a wedding. And children? No way. Spouses and children are a ball-and-chain on the mobility required along the early knowledge-career track. For this reason above all, preadults marry later than ever before in history. In 1960, the average age of marriage for women was 20 and for men, 22. Today, for the total population, the median age of first marriage is 26 for women and 28 for men. Those with a college degree are even slower to tie the knot. College-educated women marry closer to 28, and those with graduate training have a median age of marriage between 29 and 30. In parts of the Northeast and Middle Atlantic states—New York, New Jersey, Massachusetts, Rhode Island, and Washington, DC, where the percentage of college-educated people is particularly high—half of ever-married men didn't marry until they were past 30.[7]

As we have already seen, feminism gave women options. It told women they could have it all. They could have the husband, kids, career, nice house, and anything else they wanted. It even promised them that they could have it on their own timetable. The creation of the Pill gave women the freedom to choose when they wanted to start a family. The national average age of marriage shows us that women are getting married later and later. The number of women in college and in the workforce has proven that women can dream big and accomplish great things. Again, this is not all bad. But it has come at a price.

Now women are waiting to get married and to have children. Maybe you are one of them. Maybe you have been in a relationship for a while now and the only thing keeping you from getting married is that you just want to get to that next promotion before you settle down. My friend from the beginning of the chapter felt that way. She was afraid that marriage would keep her from getting ahead in her career. Or maybe you want to finish school, and you just don't see how marriage and graduating with honors would work together. Or maybe you are happily married and have been for a number of years. You really enjoy your dual-income, no-kid lifestyle and are a little fearful about what a little bundle of joy might do to the well-oiled machine of your marriage. Maybe you feel like you can't get ahead in life, and adding a child to the mix seems like too much. You want kids, you just want to feel a bit more settled first. You want to finish your graduate degree. You want to gain more work experience. You want to really feel ready, you know?

I will let you in on a little secret. You are *never* ready for marriage and children. Getting married and having kids are the most life-altering, soul-enriching, exhausting, sanctifying, crazy, wonderful things you will ever do. And they are gifts from God.

I don't think everyone should immediately go out, find a husband, and start making babies. But I do think that one of the subtle ways feminism has affected our psyches, even the most conservative among us, is in our "just wait until you're ready" mentality. By telling women they can have it all, by giving women endless choices, feminism has sold many women a bill of goods. Feminism promises freedom to have what you want when you want it. But biology doesn't have the same freedom, and there are limits to what your body can do as you age. Part of being human is recognizing that age, life circumstances, and our very bodies have limits.

The truth is, sometimes marriage and children can't wait. What so many women are sadly finding today is that the pool of men dries up in their thirties, and their biological clocks don't pause so they can advance their career in their twenties. The reality is that God created us to be married and to be fruitful and multiply. Now, I'm not going to dictate how many kids each of us should have. That's a personal decision to be made through prayer and seeking God's direction, and there are a variety of circumstances that will determine the makeup of each family. You also will never hear me say that singleness is bad. Many godly men and women are called to singleness. You will find no passages in the Bible that say everyone should get married. Nor will you find instructions on how many children to have and how to space them apart. But the Bible is clear on this: marriage and children are good things (Gen. 2:22–24; Ps. 127:3–5; Prov. 5:18–19; 18:22; Mark 9:36–37; Heb. 13:4).

You are probably already aware that our culture does not value marriage and children much. As Christians, we have the unique opportunity to say the opposite. So ask yourself and ponder this question: Am I acting like the world in how I approach men, marriage, and children?

If we waited until we were perfectly ready for marriage and children we would never take the next step. We are never ready. And in the moment that we think we are, God shows us how foolish that thinking is. God is in the business of taking weak people and giving them the strength that only he can supply (2 Cor. 12:9). Marriages are made by the abundant grace of God. Children are born, raised, and cared for by the mercy of a God who cares for us and our little ones. Maybe you are terrified by the prospect of being a wife and mother. Know this, dear sister: God has your back. The same God who created marriage and creates little babes is the one who will keep you as you follow him down this road. He will not abandon you. He has equipped you and given you everything you need to follow him.

It's true: women do want a lot. And depending on life circumstances, those wants change all of the time. But one thing is for sure:

while feminism has given women an abundance of options, it hasn't given them everything they were hoping for. The reality of sin and the fallen world shows us that not every woman will get what she wants out of life.

The great hope is that no amount of sin, personal ambition, feminism, or even good desires will change God's good design for women. As Christian women, we can recover how we relate to men and children regardless of our season of life because we know that the truth of God's Word is timeless and relevant for us all.

Restoration in My Life

As human beings, we are created to live in relation to one another. This includes our relationships with men and children. Parts of feminist ideology sought to divorce women from these relationships, treating men as useless and children as burdensome. God's Word says otherwise.

For the Single Woman

Regardless of your stage in life, grow in godliness. Even if you never marry, or if you get married much later in life, you will *never* regret the time you spent working on your own walk with the Lord.

How do you relate to the men in your life? Do you encourage them or treat them with disdain? Do you respect them as fellow image-bearers and coheirs with Christ? How do you relate to your pastor and elders? Do you respect their authority over you? Do you seek their counsel and instruction? Do you know a godly, older woman? If you do, try getting to know her better and observing her life. If you don't, ask God to open doors for you to start a friendship with an older woman you can learn from. How do you relate to your boss? Male or female, we are all under authority. So regardless of your boss's gender, how you relate to the authority over you will tell you a lot about your own heart. How do you view marriage?

Does marriage seem like a hindrance to your future plans? If so, ask God to give you a bigger view of marriage.

Perhaps you are thinking that your singleness has very little to do with children. I assure you, it has a lot to do with children. Jesus, who also was single, welcomed children (Luke 18:16). You don't have to be the first to sign up for children's ministry or babysitting to have a welcoming heart toward children. But you should value them. Maybe you have nieces or nephews who would love some time with their aunt. Maybe you enjoy rocking babies or teaching toddlers about Jesus; your church nursery could surely use you on Sunday mornings. Maybe your local crisis pregnancy center needs volunteers. As a Christian woman, you should value children, and there are many to go around.

For the Married and Childless Woman

Growing in godliness is key to walking this sometimes painful road of life. God's grace is sufficient for everything we face, whether it's a fear of having children or a desire for children that is yet to be realized. Whatever your profession, ask God to help you to do your work with all of your might. Perhaps you have a strong desire to nurture others or you feel that your gifts are not being used because you have no children. So many people need grace and comfort. Seek them out. Do you know a godly older woman who you can learn from? You were not made to walk this road alone. Do you know of children who need the nurturing care that you can provide? Ask God to reveal opportunities where you can extend Christ's love to them. Are you afraid of children? Ask God to give you a biblical understanding of children and the blessing that they are. Maybe there is a family in your church that you can get to know better. Interaction with children might not make you become a lover of babies, but it will help with fear of the unknown.

For the Married Woman with Children

Do you find your identity in your husband and children? Does your mood rise and fall on the condition of your family on any given day? It is easy in this season of life to feel as though we have "arrived" as Christian women. But we are just as susceptible to finding our identity in something other than Christ. Maybe you don't find your identity in your husband and children, but you do sometimes resent them. You remember life as a single woman or before you and your husband had children, and you look back with longing at the time of freedom. Your family is slowly becoming less appealing as you watch your single friends enjoy seemingly endless amounts of free time. Don't believe the culture's lie that says you are the most important being in your universe. Christ came to serve, not to be served (Matt. 20:28). We do likewise. The call to follow Christ is a call to decrease in our own quest for self-glory and to gladly accept his increasing glory in our lives. This means we must daily die to ourselves, rather than daily look for a way to escape the chaos of our own lives. We are doing important things in our homes every day. They might seem mundane and meaningless, but they serve an eternal purpose.

Study Questions

1. How have you experienced the tension of wanting to be autonomous but also wanting "men to be men"?

2. How can you practice encouragement and patience with men in your season of life?

3. How do you see the "just wait" attitude toward getting married and having children displayed in the church? How do you see it in your own heart?

4. What would understanding God's design for you as a woman look like in your current place in life regarding men and children?

3

Do We Have to Talk about Submission?

The images on the screen were all too familiar. I knew I had witnessed this very scene before, though with different characters and in a different setting. Yet I still sat mesmerized. As the minutes passed, my heart began to beat a little faster. My emotions were stirred, nearly to the point of tears. I was hooked.

I was watching a chick-flick.

We are all familiar with "the scene," right? The female character is stuck in a dead-end relationship with a guy who won't commit. She travels across the world to keep said guy, who is aloof to her needs and wants. Somewhere along the way, she meets a dashing, handsome, sensitive man whom she bickers with at first, but eventually falls madly in love with because he understands her every need, unlike her aloof boyfriend. And then comes the moment of truth. Should she stay with Mr. Noncommittal or marry Mr. Wonderful? After much agonizing, Mr. Wonderful wins and they live happily ever after in (either marital or nonmarital) bliss. Regardless of their marital status, they are together and the movie patrons are pleased, including myself.

Now, I'm not going to lie. I enjoy a good romantic comedy.

I also like a good ending, preferably one where everyone I like ends up happy and married. But have you ever noticed what the constant up-and-down of a whirlwind movie romance does to your own understanding of romance and marriage?

Marriage? Not for Me

I used to have a love/hate relationship with marriage. I swooned at the latest romcoms, daydreamed about Mr. Darcy, and secretly hoped someone would sweep me off my feet. But the thought of being tied down to one man forever terrified me. What if I stopped loving him one day? Or worse, what if he stopped loving me? What if I had to give up my dreams in order to be married? Conceptually, I liked the idea of marriage. I liked men, and I liked their companionship and affection. I didn't enjoy being alone for any length of time, but I really liked my freedom. Now don't get me wrong. I didn't at all mind having a man interested in me. What girl doesn't? But the mention of marriage got me all bothered. The truth is I was scared. I was scared to give myself to someone. Scared to lose my identity. Scared to lose myself, really.

I don't think my old fears are unique. Christina really likes her boyfriend. They have been together for a while. He loves Jesus. He has a good job. they both genuinely like being around each other. But when he talks about marriage, she gets antsy. She loves him, and the idea of marriage really appeals to her. But it's just that—an idea. In reality, the commitment of marriage terrifies her. *What if I have to give up my graduate work? What if I have to move? What if I fall out of love with him? It's all so permanent . . . so lifelong.*

Danielle's feelings toward marriage aren't rooted in fear. She doesn't have anything against marriage; she just isn't interested. She doesn't want a boyfriend, at least not a serious one. And she definitely doesn't want to get married. She would rather keep her steady string of interested men at arm's length, enjoying the attention they give her but never really getting too close. Her career is her marriage. Marriage is just not for her.

Mary has an entirely different approach to marriage. She watches every new romcom or drama with bated breath, hoping that one day the stories she watches on the screen will come true in her own life. Whenever a guy asks her out, she starts planning her wedding before the first date even ends. And if she gets a second date, she's ready for the ring. Marriage has always been on her radar. She can hardly wait to be the one to walk down the aisle to Mr. Wonderful.

These fictional tales are merely examples of the myriad of feelings toward marriage a woman can have. In many respects, marriage isn't too popular in our current culture. Headlines reveal that if marriage isn't on a path to becoming obsolete, it most certainly is being redefined. Ask any random people on the street to define marriage, and you will get vastly different answers.

Not surprisingly, feminist thinking has had an impact on how we view marriage. When Betty Friedan burst on the scene with her book *The Feminine Mystique,* she challenged the 1950s stereotype that was alive and thriving in America. She wanted women to be free of the mess that marriage caused them: isolation, lack of self-awareness, and bondage to their husbands and children. Enter Gloria Steinem. Steinem, the founder of *Ms. Magazine,* famously proclaimed that she would never marry. While she did eventually marry later in life, even then she was quick to define marriage on her own terms.[1] Now here we are in the twenty-first century and marriage rates in America are at an all-time low. We could attribute the decline to a number of things, including the increase in couples living together, the rampant sexual immorality in our culture, or the high number of divorces. But it is worth mentioning that feminism has had something to do with this decline in marriage. Feminism gave women many good options. But when Friedan and other second-wave feminists stated that attachment to a man was a hindrance to personal autonomy and self-awareness, marriage became a lower priority for the impressionable women who were coming up after them.

The Value of Marriage

Regardless of your relationship status right now, you cannot deny that marriage is important. If you are single and tempted to tune me out because you think this chapter surely can't relate to you, I hope you will stick with me. Hebrews 13:4 says that marriage is to be held in honor by all. We do well to understand why marriage is important, regardless of our marital status. Even if you're single, you can faithfully hold marriage in high honor by your response to friends who get married, your encouragement of your married friends, and your attitude toward marriage in general. It is easy to grow jaded about marriage when everyone around you is partaking in the marital fun and you are left alone yet again on a Friday night. But the "all" in Hebrews 13:4 applies to *everyone,* married or single. This verse has in view God's purpose for marriage.

So take heart, single sister. This chapter is for you, too.

The Purpose of Marriage

Men and women have been getting married for thousands of years. Few things cross cultures like marriage, though certainly some differences exist. Some cultures, such as those in less developed countries, have higher rates of marriage. Some practice polygamy. Some have liberal divorce laws. Others are more restrictive. But the truth remains that people have been getting married in a variety of settings and cultures for a long time.

As Christians, we believe that marriage is an institution that God created (Gen. 2:18–25; Mark 10:6–9). Because of that, he gets to define it. Right now in America, the definition of marriage is rapidly changing—and all over the world, really. Before we understand how God designed men and women to relate in marriage, we have to first understand his purposes in creating the institution.

The Bible talks about marriage repeatedly, from the very beginning in Genesis to the final marriage in Revelation. But we get a clear understanding of God's purpose for marriage from the book of Ephesians.

> Wives, submit to your own husbands, as to the Lord. For the husband is the head of the wife even as Christ is the head of the church, his body, and is himself its Savior. Now as the church submits to Christ, so also wives should submit in everything to their husbands.
>
> Husbands, love your wives, as Christ loved the church and gave himself up for her, that he might sanctify her, having cleansed her by the washing of water with the word, so that he might present the church to himself in splendor, without spot or wrinkle or any such thing, that she might be holy and without blemish. In the same way husbands should love their wives as their own bodies. He who loves his wife loves himself. For no one ever hated his own flesh, but nourishes and cherishes it, just as Christ does the church, because we are members of his body. "Therefore a man shall leave his father and mother and hold fast to his wife, and the two shall become one flesh." This mystery is profound, and I am saying that it refers to Christ and the church. However, let each one of you love his wife as himself, and let the wife see that she respects her husband. (Eph. 5:22–33)

Here, Paul gives directives to both husbands and wives for a distinct purpose—to mirror the relationship between Christ and his bride, the church. The marriage relationship does not exist solely to make a couple feel good. It exists to tell a story about the pivotal event of human history—our salvation.

Paul commands husbands to love their wives in the very way that Christ loved us. A husband is to sacrifice for his wife. He is to lead her. He is to work with all of his might to help her grow in godliness so that on the last day God will look at her and say, "Well done, good and faithful servant." In the marital relationship, a godly husband has his wife's good in mind as he leads her, in the same way that Christ always has our good in mind as he leads us toward maturity.

The Dreaded *S* Word

We can't get very far in our discussion of marriage without talking about the big elephant in the room.

Submission.

Every few months, marriage is all the rage in the media. The morning talk shows bring in trusted "experts" for a discussion on what makes a marriage work. Sometimes the answer is found in sharing the chores around the house. Sometimes it's taking turns and listening to one another. And other times you might get a stray expert who actually thinks a wife's submission is the key to marital bliss. Usually, that sets off a firestorm. The talk show hosts (especially the women) can't fathom a woman who would submit to anyone, let alone a man. Eventually the story subsides, and another expert comes along with entirely new data supporting his or her keys to a happy marriage. And the culture waits expectantly for the results of the latest poll or new data telling us what will make us happy.

In many circles, if you bring up the topic of submission, you're looking to pick a fight. But submission is one of those often caricatured, rarely understood parts of the Christian life.

In fact, as I was writing this chapter, former child TV star Candace Cameron Bure (known for her role on the sitcom *Full House*) was under a media microscope for her statement that she submits to her husband in their marriage. Bure, a Christian, defined submitting to her husband in this way: "The definition I'm using with the word 'submissive' is the biblical definition of that. So, it is meekness, it is not weakness. It is strength under control, it is bridled strength."[2]

The journalist who interviewed her could not believe what she was hearing. Submission? In these modern, postfeminist times? As Bure demonstrated in her statement, we must clearly understand what we mean when we speak about submission.

The Basis for Submission

It's easy to find caricatures of submission. It's not a popular word. Before we look at the basis for submission, let's look at some common caricatures.

The Doormat

Maybe you have heard (or believe) this one. Anytime someone mentions the word *submission*, you bristle. You see submission as stripping a woman of her brain. Submission to you means that a woman never says anything, even when saying something would protect someone else or prevent sin. People who see submission as a means to make women brainless doormats think it takes away a woman's voice and removes her ability to have opinions. She is simply supposed to sit there and look pretty. A woman is always compelled to obey her husband, praise her husband, and never utter a critical word to her husband regardless of his treatment of her (including abuse and other sinful behavior).

The Personality Killer

Others see submission as limiting a woman's personality. They view some women as easily falling in line with submission, but that's owing to their specific personalities. For a woman who has a stronger personality than her husband, submission is a hindrance to her flourishing. Submission, by this definition, has no room for a strong, boisterous personality. It sees the "gentle and quiet spirit" as a personality trait, and one that not every woman can conceivably conform to. Biblical submission takes a woman and removes her personality, unless of course she is naturally the quiet and silent type. There is no room for anyone else in biblical submission.

When Daniel and I were in premarital counseling, the pastor asked me what my basis for submission was. At the time, God had worked in my heart and provided godly men and women who taught me the biblical pattern of submission. But I was caught off guard by the question. By God's grace, I had become convinced that his Word taught that as a wife I should submit to my husband, but I wasn't expecting to be asked the question in the weeks prior to getting married. But it was an important issue that I needed to be clear on before I walked down the aisle.

What would you say? Would you say that you submit because your husband (or future husband) possesses wonderful leadership qualities? Or because he cares for you and listens to your opinions and you love him dearly? While those are all good reasons to submit, they won't sustain you over the long haul. Your husband won't always display those wonderful leadership qualities you so admire now. Your husband won't always love and lead you like he should. But submission is still commanded.

While I didn't fully understand what the pastor was asking me, and wouldn't until after I said "I do," I answered by saying that when I submit to Daniel, I am ultimately submitting to God. I saw that in Ephesians 5, Paul exhorts Christian wives to submit to their husbands as they submit to Christ. Christ's leadership is the basis for submitting to our husbands—not any character trait they might possess at the moment. Submission is a willing decision to bridle your strength out of respect for your husband, but ultimately out of obedience to God and reverence for his Word.

Our ability to submit in marriage is rooted in our relationship to God. We submit to our husbands because we know we are ultimately submitting to God and his rightful authority over us and our marriage. Submission is also an act of trusting in God and his work in our lives. He has established our husbands as the authority, therefore we can submit to our husbands because we trust that the work God began in them will be carried to completion on the final day (Phil. 1:6). Submission is not about the man. It's about the God-man.

It's important to note that everyone is called to some form of submission. Children submit to parents (Eph. 6:1; Col. 3:20). Slaves submit to masters (Eph. 6:5; 1 Pet. 2:18). We all submit to God and his Word (1 Pet. 5:6).

Sometimes when we talk about submission, we speak in lofty terms. But submission is really about sacrifice. All Christians are called to some form of sacrifice. When men lead their wives like Christ, they are sacrificing their desires for the good of another.

When wives submit, they are sacrificing their "rights" in obedience to Christ. But it's not always a cakewalk.

Consider Sarah. Peter praises her in 1 Peter 3 for her obedience to Abraham, but have you ever considered the cost of her obedience? When God called Abraham (then named Abram) to leave his country, Sarah (then Sarai) went along with him (Genesis 11). Needless to say, this was in the pre–cell-phone, pre-Skype, pre-snail mail ancient Near East. When Sarah left, it was for good. And it wasn't a smooth journey. Twice Abraham put her in harm's way by lying about her identity as his wife (Gen. 12:10–20; 20:1–18). On top of that, she was barren, and while God promised her a child, she grew impatient with the wait (Genesis 16). Sarah herself was hardly a model for perfect obedience, just like her husband. So why does Peter praise her? Because she hoped in God (1 Pet. 3:5). Her standing as a godly woman, and a model for us to follow, is rooted in her steadfast hope in the God who held her life in his hands, even if it took her (and Abraham) a while to trust God completely. So take heart, sister. If you struggle with the biblical command to submit to your husband, know that you are in good company. We all struggle. But God is not finished with you. The God who started the work in Sarah (and in you) is faithful to complete it (Phil. 1:6).

Submission and Jesus

Our husbands will fail us. No one knew that more than Sarah, right? They will not lead like God commanded them to. They will not always love us like Christ. They will hurt us deeply. And we will not submit perfectly. Thankfully, we are not left to ourselves.

Consider the Savior. His sinless life gives us a beautiful depiction of what God intended for submission. Christ had every right to exert his power and extol his competency as God, yet he humbled himself, bridled his strength and authority, and submitted to the Father (Phil. 2:6–8). If for a moment he had thrown up his hands and said, "I am God. I deserve better than this," we would all be lost. He submitted all the way to the cross, not because it was easy, and not because it gave him the most praise, but because he trusted in the sovereign, good will of the Father.

The Gospels give us a glimpse into this joyful submission of Christ:

> And he withdrew from them about a stone's throw, and knelt down and prayed, saying, "Father, if you are willing, remove this cup from me. Nevertheless, not my will, but yours, be done." (Luke 22:41–42)

> Father, I desire that they also, whom you have given me, may be with me where I am, to see my glory that you have given me because you loved me before the foundation of the world. O righteous Father, even though the world does not know you, I know you, and these know that you have sent me. I made known to them your name, and I will continue to make it known, that the love with which you have loved me may be in them, and I in them." (John 17:24–26)

Did you catch that? Complete trust. Utmost respect. Obedience to authority. Utter devotion. Does submission feel overwhelming to you? Does it feel impossible? It is. But that is why Christ did it all for us. He is our perfect model of submission. But he is so much more than that. He is our righteousness, so when we fail to yield to rightful authority (whomever that may be), we have grace and an advocate before the Father. He also promises to us the power to obey him and his commands through his Spirit (2 Cor. 1:21–22).

What Submission Isn't

One of the loudest arguments against submission is that it makes women into doormats. In our society we praise autonomy and personal freedom. The very notion that anyone would willingly place herself under anyone is a foreign concept. Our American values of independence and democracy make submission all the more difficult to swallow. The feminist movement gave women a loud voice in society, and now when people hear words like *subordination, submission,* and *obedience,* everyone gets a little uneasy. Images of slavery, property, and weak women blast across our minds. Modern women submit to no one, especially to men. While I was working on this chapter, I read an interview about a remake of the film *Rosemary's Baby.* In the interview the lead actress revealed that she was pleased with the departure of her character from the submissive, obedient wife of the original movie.[3] She was appalled that in 2014 anyone would expect that of a wife anyway. And in 2011, when Kate Middleton married Prince William of England, few were surprised that she chose not to say the word *obey* in her wedding vows.[4]

I can see how the call to submission might make a woman squirm, especially when it is associated with weakness and a lack of voice. Who wants to be a doormat, right? Even in evangelicalism, submission gets a bad rap. So it is helpful to explain what submission is not, especially in light of the biblical definition.

One of the biggest misunderstandings of submission is that it makes women submissive to all men everywhere, essentially saying that Scripture commands us to submit to our best friend's husband, our neighbor, or even our younger brother. Biblical submission does not require women to submit to all men all the time. For example, if you have a boyfriend, you are not biblically required to submit to him. In fact, you shouldn't submit to him. How do we know this? First Peter 3:1 says that wives are to submit to their "*own husbands.*" And the last time I checked, your boyfriend isn't your husband. Russell Moore says that when the Bible tells women to submit to their own husbands, it is effectively telling them to refuse to submit to other men around them, that is, not to give their hearts and lives away to men who are not worthy of their affections. He has this helpful exhortation regarding submission:

> Sisters, there is no biblical category for "boyfriend" or "lover," and you owe such designation no submission. In fact, to be submissive to your future husband you must stand back and evaluate, with rigid scrutiny, "Is this the one who is to come,

> or is there another?" That requires an emotional and physical distance until there is a lifelong covenant made, until you stand before one who is your "own husband."
>
> Wives, submit yourselves to your husbands as unto the Lord. Yes and Amen. But, women, stop submitting to men.[5]

Another misunderstanding of submission is that it makes women more susceptible to abuse. Biblical submission is not submitting to abuse or sin. This is crucial. True biblical submission actually leads to human flourishing, not withering. But sadly the biblical concept of submission is often distorted for unjust gain. Submission and Christ-honoring leadership go together. Christ *never* wields his power by keeping his bride under his thumb. He never abuses her or leads her into sin. Biblical submission, because it is rooted in submission to God as our supreme authority, is always done with God's Word in view. God values women. He loves them. He will stop at nothing to protect them. Submission is never done under compulsion or force. It is a choice, made because we love God and we love his Word. We must never confuse submission with force and power struggles.

There Is Room for Your Personality

When I was in seminary, my girlfriends and I had a running joke. Whenever one of us got angry or frustrated with a situation, the others would chide her that she wasn't exhibiting her "gentle and quiet spirit." Usually we would banter back and forth about her Jezebel ways, joking that upstanding Christian men wanted a submissive spirit, and her loud antics were hardly meeting that mark.

All joking aside, perhaps when you think about submission, you envision a certain kind of woman. She is quiet. She is soft-spoken. She is always compliant and nice. But when you look in the mirror, or worse, hear yourself talk, you feel anything but gentle and quiet.

Usually, talk of submission and a gentle and quiet spirit go hand in hand. And they should. To be submissive requires a level of resignation and trust that characterizes a biblical woman. In fact, Peter put them all together too:

> Likewise, wives, be subject to your own husbands, so that even if some do not obey the word, they may be won without a word by the conduct of their wives, when they see your respectful and pure conduct. Do not let your adorning be external—the braiding of hair and the putting on of gold jewelry, or the clothing you wear—but let your adorning be the hidden person of the heart with the imperishable beauty of a gentle and quiet spirit, which in God's sight is very precious. For this is how the holy women who hoped in God used to adorn themselves, by submitting to their own husbands, as Sarah obeyed Abraham, calling him lord. And you are her children, if you do good and do not fear anything that is frightening. (1 Pet. 3:1–6)

So what is this submissive spirit all about, anyway?

Being a godly woman does not require a one-size-fits-all personality. Of course, with every personality there are avenues for sin, but the spirit Peter refers to is not a personality. It is a disposition toward God. Sarah's spirit was praised because she hoped in God, not because she checked off a personality trait in a box. In fact, we learn very little about her personality in the Bible.

Consider Emma. She has never been defined as the quiet type. Even in her earliest school days, it was a struggle to keep her mouth shut in class. She loves people, and she loves talking to them. Her friends feel comfortable around her because she is always available to have a conversation. When she walks into a room of strangers, she sees potential friends. Emma is known for her vibrant personality and passionate conversations.

Abigail is Emma's older sister. Even though they share the same gene pool, they couldn't be more different from one another. Unlike Emma, Abigail is more of an introvert. She loves people, but also needs time alone to recharge and think. In a crowded room, you will often find Abigail talking with one person or simply listening in on another conversation. She is quiet and reserved and takes time to get to know people.

Which of these two sisters possesses a gentle and quiet spirit?

They both can. Here is what I mean.

Abigail and Emma's mom was diagnosed with cancer shortly after Abigail got married. Emma was in the process of planning her own wedding when she received the devastating news that her mother's cancer was terminal. They didn't have much time left with her, and she likely would not see Emma walk down the aisle. Both daughters were devastated. Abigail was faced with the dashed hopes of never seeing her children with her mother. Emma was faced with the broken dream of her mother not being with her on her wedding day. This was a hard providence for their entire family. In the midst of their grief over their mother's impending death, both sisters demonstrated a resolute trust in God—a gentle and quiet spirit. Instead of responding like Job's wife, who told Job to "curse God and die" (Job 2:9), Abigail and Emma entrusted their very dreams for their future to the God they know does all things well. Their very souls rested in God's purposes for their lives, even in grief. They wept and grieved, but they also clung to God alone. Their lives were a beautiful testimony to the faithfulness of God in the midst of great sadness.

Emma, with her outgoing and talkative personality, is just as able to possess a gentle and quiet spirit as her quiet and reserved sister, Abigail, because a gentle and quiet spirit is rooted in trusting God, not personality.

I remember when this was clearly solidified for me. An older, godly woman was interviewing me for a missions trip. She served in leadership for the women of our church, was well-versed in the Scriptures, and was prepared to lead a trip to an orphanage in Jamaica. As she talked with me about my strengths and weaknesses, I expressed concern that I felt that I was at times too opinionated. I had tried to master what I thought was a gentle and quiet spirit, yet always found my opinionated and loud personality getting in the way. I will never forget her answer: "You are not opinionated, Courtney. You have conviction. *Opinionated* implies you have no thought behind voicing your opinions. *Conviction* is rooted in knowing God and his Word. Women should have conviction." I was floored. By God's grace she continued to pour into my life and show me how a gentle and quiet spirit was marked mostly by trusting in God and his promises, not my personality. She was a woman with conviction who was not afraid to take a stand on them. She possessed great courage in the face of great difficulty. Yet I watched her willingly yield to her husband, who came on our trip to serve us as we cared for orphans. I watched her willingly listen to him and submit to his leadership even as she led us to care for the vulnerable.

Do you see the pattern here? Submission is only possible if we have a resolute trust in God.

What does this mean for you? First, know your personality. Because you and I are sinners, we struggle to live the way God called us to. I have an expressive, opinionated, talkative personality. And I come from a long line of expressive women. We are hardly doormats. Ask our husbands. My struggle with submission looks much different than a woman with a quieter, less talkative personality. But God is in the business of redeeming personalities. Every last one of them.

One way we know that biblical submission is hardly a blueprint for doormat status is because God shows us that marriage is a beautiful picture of a relationship of friends and equals. When Adam saw Eve for the first time, he didn't praise God for giving him a servant to meet his every need. He praised God for giving him an equal from his very flesh. He was delighted with her. Proverbs 31:11 shows us that a godly woman's husband trusts her. She is a beloved help to him. How can a husband trust and, for that matter, delight in a doormat? How can a husband trust a wife if she does not willingly share her thoughts, dreams, and opinions with him?

As women who desire to grow in godliness, we would do well to strive to be trustworthy. The greatest thing you can do right now, whether married or single, is to ask God to make you into a woman who is faithful, trustworthy, and strong.

Submission and the Single

If you are single, you may be wondering what all this submission talk has to do with you. Maybe you want to be married, and my harping on submission only highlights the gaping man-shaped hole in your life. Maybe marriage isn't on your radar, and talk about submission sounds like a foreign language from a country you have no intention of visiting. You aren't familiar with it, and probably will never need to use it.

But submission is not just a marriage issue. If submission in marriage is ultimately about our submission to God—and it is—then submission matters for everyone. If a gentle and quiet spirit is ultimately marked by a trust in God, then it matters for all of us. We are all under some degree of authority. From the toddler with her parents to the corporate executive with her board of directors, authority structures are a natural part of life. Even as Christians we are called to submit to our pastors, governmental officials, and employers (Rom. 13:1–7; Heb. 13:17; 1 Pet. 2:13–17). And what if it is God's plan that you marry one day? A woman who has never learned to submit over the course of her life will have a very hard time just turning it on the day she gets married.

So while you might not be in a position to submit to a man as your husband, you probably have some authority structure over you. And as a Christian, submission to Christ as his blood-bought bride is your basis for all other forms of submission.

Is That *Really* What That Means?

Some have said that Paul's commands do not ultimately mean that wives are to submit to their husbands in the way that I have just described. For years, scholars have debated Paul and Peter's words, challenging them on the basis of everything from cultural context to flat out saying submission cannot and does not mean what we think it does.[6]

As I've tried to show throughout this book, God's plans are not random. When he created Adam and Eve, he had a purpose in mind—to display his glory throughout his creation. This is why he created us in his image. How we act has implications. Whenever the biblical writers talk about marriage, gender, and even headship and submission, they are always referring back to the original creation account in Genesis 1–2. When we talk about gender roles in marriage and God's design for men and women, these ideas are not arbitrary or cultural constructs. They are rooted in God's intent for humanity. The Bible presents a postfall world where men and women hardly act in line with God's plan for them. Our world today is no exception. And Christ came to redeem all of it.

At the end of the day, we must take God at his word. Did he have a purpose when he created us male and female? Did he have a purpose when he created marriage, with its differing roles? I believe that he did.

When Submission Isn't Easy

What about the times when submitting to your husband feels like everything *but* a joy and a privilege? What do you do when he asks you to follow him and trust him, and you want to do the exact opposite? (I want to be clear that I am not talking about times when a husband asks his wife to follow him into sin or when a husband is sinfully exerting his own rights and leadership. That kind of "leadership" is far from the biblical pattern for headship and submission.)

Like many new brides, I entered marriage with rose-colored glasses. Prior to getting married I had studied the biblical passages about marriage, and I thought I had the whole submission thing down. In fact, I couldn't wait to apply all I had learned. I think it's safe to say that God knew my pride needed a good humbling! And so it was in this arrogant spirit that I began my married life.

I quickly learned that it's easy to talk about headship and submission in theoretical terms. When we hear it addressed at conferences and in Sunday morning sermons, we nod our heads in agreement and think to ourselves, *That can't be that hard, right?*

But what about when you and your husband have talked through an issue and you are at an impasse? You don't know where to go from there. You want one thing and he wants the other. What do you do?

It didn't take long for such a situation to arise in my marriage. We had only been married a few months when my husband asked me to trust him with something that I held very dear. He was asking me to drop out of seminary. His decision to go against my desires felt like a stab in the back. I thought he was against me, and sadly I treated him that way too. *How could this be happening,* I thought. *If he loved me, he would give me everything I want, right?* Even though I believed submission was biblical—even though I believed that following his leadership was God's plan—I was angry. It was as if every fear I ever had about marriage was being realized in this one moment

Let me be clear: my husband didn't think I wasn't qualified or gifted to go to seminary. It wasn't that he didn't believe in me. But he knew our budget. And he knew we couldn't make it work with both of us in seminary. One of us had to drop out, and he appealed to our shared beliefs regarding our future, and he asked me to trust him. He asked me to trust that God would honor our desire to be financially wise and my ultimate trust in his leadership. He knew that I, like him, believed that the Bible taught that men are called to be the primary providers of the family. If we were going to be obedient to that calling, then he would need to finish seminary in order to move forward in his career path. He knew that I, like him, believed that the pastorate was reserved for men. While we both firmly believed seminary to be beneficial for women, we knew that in order to be faithful to the Scriptures, and keep our bank account from dwindling, I would need to drop out.

At first I was defiant. How could he ask me to abandon my dream? How could he expect me to support him through seminary, knowing that with every theological book he read, paper he wrote, and Greek word he parsed, I would desperately long to do the exact same thing? In my mind obeying him meant denying myself. It meant denying what I wanted and hoped for. It meant a life of working a nine-to-five job I hated while he got to do the fun stuff.

Then one day Daniel said, "You know that I am *for* you, Court, don't you?" His care for me, and his decision to lead our family, was the perfect expression of his love and commitment to me. He knew that his responsibility before God was a serious one, and he didn't take these decisions lightly or without prayer. What I failed to see was that his leadership of our home was for my good, not my evil. We weren't pitted against each other—but I wasn't autonomous either.

In my deepest moments of despair over what my marriage was doing to my dreams, I was missing something crucial about God's call on my life to submit to my husband. Before I got married, submission seemed like such a noble thing. I wanted to be the godly wife who always submitted to her husband with joy. But when the rubber met the road, it was a lot harder than I anticipated. And the little voice of feminism spoke quietly in my ears, challenging me to seek my own rights rather than lay them down for another.

Submission turned from a flippant idea to a hard-to-live reality. I learned that mastering submission is not one more notch to earn in my belt of godly womanhood. Rather, submission is a lifelong process of daily dying to myself and my wants for the good of another. After talking through every aspect of the decision and hearing every angle, at the end of the day I had to trust that God had my back, and my husband did, too.

But what about when you both think your side is correct? What happens when you've reached a stalemate? This will likely happen at some point over the course of your marriage. You have voiced your side. Your husband has voiced his. And you still can't agree. It's hard. Your opinion matters. Your voice is valuable. But at the end of the day your submission is ultimately to God, not your husband. God has given him the responsibility of leadership, and sometimes it means he makes a decision you don't agree with. Because you submit to God first, you can trust that God will work in your husband's life and in yours. You can trust that God has your back, even if your husband doesn't see your side as clearly as you would like him to. I'm not saying it's easy. But like so much of life, marriage is one more opportunity to daily die to ourselves and trust God for the outcome.

Before I go any farther, I think it is important to talk about when a husband is imperfect, or worse, when he is abusing his wife. Both circumstances are not owing to the biblical model of leadership and submission, but a sad and sinful distortion of what God designed to be good. In the case of an imperfect husband (and we all will face this to varying degrees), we can first pray that God would change his heart. But we also must love him as his sister in Christ. Submission does not mean condoning sin in the lives of our husbands. As fellow believers, we have a responsibility to love our husbands well by pointing out sinful patterns that are not changing (Matt. 18:15–16). If he refuses to change, then you are free to ask your pastors or elders to intervene in his life (v. 17).

If you are in an abusive marriage, please know that you are not biblically required to submit to abuse. First and foremost, protect yourself and family from the abuse you are receiving. No amount of submission will protect you from the abuse. Submission is not the problem. Your husband's sin is. Please get help from your pastors and local authorities, and know that this abuse is not your fault.

Our pattern for submission is not a cultural construct or a throwback to June Cleaver and the 1950s happy housewife. Our pattern for submission is our Savior, who, for the joy set before him, obeyed the Father all the way to death so we wouldn't have to. We submit not ultimately to a man, but to the God-man. We submit to the very One who mastered submission on our behalf, trusting that the same work he is doing in our own life, he is doing in the life of our husbands.

God does not command things that are easy. If he did, then anyone could master his commands and we wouldn't need him. Instead he commands a level of living that is impossible because of our sinful nature. But the biblical pattern of submission seen in Scripture is not to be done in our own strength. Jesus—the one who gave us the pattern of submission—is the very one who ensures that we can submit. And even better, he paid for every sinful tantrum we throw when we don't get our way. I, for one, am thankful for that grace.

Submission is not ultimately about us, our husbands, or our little corner of marital bliss. *It's about God.* It's about the story we tell with our lives. When I submit to my husband, I am telling a watching world, even if the only ones watching are my children, what I believe about God and his work. Do I believe he ultimately has my back? Or do I need to insist on my own way? What I was doing in those early days of marriage was really saying that my way was best. I was saying that getting what I wanted mattered more than anything else.

I wish I could say that it is easier for me now to yield to God and his plan for my life. But I am still a work in progress. While I may not have finished my seminary degree, and most likely will not finish it anytime soon (if ever), I learned a valuable lesson. My husband is not my enemy. He is my friend and my partner. When I got over the fact that he was leading us to do something I didn't want at the time, I was able to see that our marriage was not some battle of the wills. I didn't need to seek my own way. My way had become his way, and vice versa. And recognizing this has had a tremendous impact on my attitude toward him and his leadership.

I'm a slow learner, unfortunately. But what I am ever increasingly thankful for is the truth that the Christ who obeyed to the cross will keep me until the end—even when submission isn't easy.

But Why Is It So Hard?

As I already shared, I learned early on that submission was not a walk in the park. While I entered marriage thinking submission was just one more notch in my "obedience to the Lord" belt, I quickly learned that submission in marriage requires a daily dying to ourselves and our own desires. It is not easy. Submitting to your husband (or even practicing rightful respect for authority premarriage) is not about learning how to say yes and doing whatever is asked of you. It requires tremendous strength—one that cannot come from inside you.

The truth is, you can't submit to your husband (or future husband) anymore than your husband (or future husband) can love you like Christ loved the church. You need a supernatural work of the One who fully understands and who perfectly submitted. Jesus Christ knows what it means to submit to rightful authority because he submitted to the Father. Jesus Christ knows what it means to love his bride sacrificially. And it is by his shed blood that we are enabled to do the very thing that we feel in our bones is completely impossible.

Marriage matters. We don't get to define it. We don't get to scoff at it and say that only weak people give up their freedom for another (like I used to). We don't get to pretend like the roles within a marriage relationship are arbitrary and meaningless. Frankly, it's not for us to decide. The beauty of a good marriage is that it points away from itself and toward the One whom marriage was always designed to mirror. When we say "I do," we are doing something far more significant than just playing dress-up in front of two hundred of our closest friends. Like our gender, our marriages tell a story about Christ and his gospel.

So while I still enjoy a good chick flick every now and then, I'm starting to realize that the romance of Hollywood is a far cry from the flesh-and-blood romance of a real marriage that images our Savior and his bride. Maybe it's just me, but when I spend a lot of my time indulging in the latest Hollywood romance, I start thinking that my greatest need is to be understood fully by a man. Who wouldn't want that? The Bible tells husbands to live with their wives in an understanding way, so I should expect nothing less, right (1 Pet. 3:7)? Sure, as long as he can expect that I will always submit to him and respect him with a happy heart. A steady, unregulated diet of romantic comedies will make me slowly dissatisfied with covenant-keeping love with and for my husband. The characters in romances tell me that *my* needs are ultimate. They tell me that relationships can be ended at anytime, especially when someone better comes along. Ultimately, they tell me a lie.

Very rarely do movies present strong, covenantal, life-long love as the relationship worth finding. Headship and submission do not make a blockbuster. Marriage has been so squandered by those inside and outside of the church that our culture doesn't see it as anything special anymore. But God, the Creator of the universe, sees it as infinitely special not because we do it right all of the time, but because it points to something far more glorious—our Christ and his bride, the church. If we really grasped the wonder of this mystery, we wouldn't want to settle for anything less in our own marriages and in the ones portrayed on our television or movie screens.

My heart is corrupt. And so is yours. Regular consumption of media that lies about God's design for our lives can have disastrous effects on our souls if we are not careful. Does it mean we never consume secular media? Of course not. But it does mean that we have a sober understanding of the fact that there is a Devil out there seeking to devour our understanding of marriage because he hates the image it represents—Christ and the church (Eph. 5:32; 1 Pet. 5:8).

Restoration in My Life

As we have seen, feminism and the shifting sands of culture have taken a toll on the biblical understanding of marriage and submission. By God's grace we have been given his Word as a means of knowing his good plan for our lives and marriages. Marriage and submission are part of this good design. Our personalities aren't hindrances on the path to becoming godly women. There is room for all of us.

For the Single Woman

Ask God to reveal areas in your life where you question or reject authority. Growing in your understanding of rightful authority will prepare you to submit in marriage or simply prepare you to live life as a Christian. We all submit to someone, married or not. Grow in your understanding of the Savior. He is your hope of submission. Learn to honor marriage even in your particular season of life. As we have seen, our culture does not respect marriage. What a testimony it would be if you held marriage in honor even as a single woman. What are some specific ways you could do this? Encourage your friends who are married or preparing to be married. Pray for them. The enemy hates marriage and will seek to attack it at every level. Ask your friends about their marriages. Don't malign marriage when others mock it or speak ill of it. Joyfully attend weddings (this can be hard, I know). You can do a lot of good to honor the marriages around you and show a watching world that God values marriage.

For the Married Woman

Prayer is crucial to growing in your marriage. Do you pray regularly for your husband and your marriage? I know that I don't pray often enough, and am regularly convicted in this area. Grow in your understanding of Christ and his righteousness. It is only through his work on your behalf that you can begin to submit to your husband. Immerse yourself in God's Word. Again, Scripture is where you will see Christ in all his glory. Christ is your only hope of change and living rightly in your marriage. Begin submitting now. You will never do it perfectly, but you can ask God for grace to respect and honor your husband's leadership even when he fails you. Again, if your husband is abusive or if you are dealing with repetitive sin issues, please get help from your local authorities (for abuse) or your pastor. The Bible never condones abuse, and you should not submit to it.

Study Questions

1. Do you struggle with the concept of submission? What specifically makes you uncomfortable with the idea? What does the biblical definition of submission look like?

2. What does God's Word have to say to our culture's current views on marriage? Refer to specific Scripture passages.

3. What is a biblical understanding of a gentle and quiet spirit? How can you demonstrate this spirit in your life?

4. Have you experienced a time when submission to authority was difficult? How did you handle the situation? What was the outcome?

5. How can you hold marriage in honor in your life right now (married or single)?

4

My Body on Display

If you have ever worked in the restaurant industry, or are familiar with the lifestyle, you know that it is hardly a place where Christ is glorified. Late nights, fast cash, and transient people often are a recipe for hard living and all that goes along with it. That was my life before Jesus found me.

I worked as a waitress and bartender in college. In the particular restaurant where I worked, the men had a special signal for when an attractive woman walked through the front door. A bartender would ring the bell in the bar. At the first chime, virtually every male server, bartender, and yes, even the managers, would stop what they were doing to partake of the eye candy, unbeknownst to the woman who came to dine and much to the chagrin of every female server, bartender, and manager. It was a Mexican restaurant, and we all had to dress the part. So as you can imagine, the female employees were hardly a match for the street-clothes wearing women who came to be waited on. Something about Mexican-themed clothing and hair that smells of fajitas just doesn't make you bell-ringing material.

This had an effect on me. Whenever I came in on my days off, I wanted to be that girl that solicited a good bell-ringing. I knew what it took, so I dressed the part. I wanted attention. I wanted love. And I wanted to be deemed the prettiest in the place—at least for that moment. I wanted the bell to ring for me.

Third-Wave Feminism and Our Bodies

Something happened in feminist thinking in the mid-1990s. Feminism used to be about protecting women from predatory men. This was why conservatives and feminists could often find themselves on the same side of many issues. As pornography sought a foothold in society, for example, both sides joined forces to fight porn and its impact on women. Such collaboration, however, now rarely occurs.

You might not identify as a third-wave feminist, or really know anyone who does, but you most likely have been exposed to it in some capacity.

Ever heard of *Sex and the City*? The popular HBO television show of the late 90s/early 2000s was in many ways a face of third-wave feminism. The show thrived on the boisterous sex lives of four female New York City friends. The women had varying levels of standards and morality, but the point was that they each got to choose their own standards. According to third-wave feminists, men have defined sexuality for women for too long. Women should, and now do, have the right to own and control their bodies and their sexuality. If a woman wants to ask a man out and sleep with him on the first date, she has that right. If a woman wants to flaunt her body through revealing clothing, it's her right. And consider the common refrain of the abortion movement: no one has the right to tell a woman what she can or cannot do with her own body. Sexual freedom as defined by third-wave feminism was the last great frontier for women's issues. A quick survey of the covers of recent women's magazines reveals our attitudes toward sexuality today (these are ones suitable for reprint):

- "Learn the Secrets He Is Afraid to Tell You but Secretly Wants in Bed"
- "How to Be Sexy for Your Man"
- "10 Beauty Tips That Will Make You Look Like a Celebrity"

In many ways, beauty is now synonymous with sex. Because sex sells and helps women get ahead, beauty is now defined by our sexuality. As Christian women, we know there is a better definition of beauty, one that is not defined by sexuality or a changing culture. It is defined by God.

Third-wave feminism was perfectly poised to emerge in a post-modern society, where truth, gender, and sexuality no longer find their meaning in absolutes. You may not even realize it, but the complete redefinition of sexuality, gender, and morality is in part a product of third-wave feminism. Freedom of choice now means the freedom to choose any expression of love and morality—and not be judged for it.

One of the lasting impacts of third-wave feminism is that sex is now the power tool that women wield to show their equality and identity. In a recent interview concerning her brash nudity on the show *Girls*, Lena Dunham defended her choice to shed it all for the cameras as exactly that—her choice.

> In the moment, Dunham herself spoke clearly about her position on the nudity, saying it is "a realistic expression of what it's like to be alive. But I totally get it. If you're not into me, that's your problem and you're going to have to work that out with professionals," she retorted. And later, fellow EP Jenni Konner interrupted her response to another question to add, "I literally was spacing out because I'm in such a rage spiral about that guy," she said pointing to the question-asker. "I was just looking at him and going into this rage [over] this idea that you would talk to a woman like that and accuse a woman of showing her body too much. The idea it just makes me sort of sick."[1]

To suggest that women should follow a particular standard of modesty, morality, or ethics regarding their own bodies is offensive (even to the point of being sickening) to this budding generation of feminists.

Dunham is not alone. Jessica Valenti, a prominent figure in third-wave feminism, has made it her mission to dismantle the abstinence and purity argument, citing that it actually makes girls more promiscuous and places unfair attention on the girls as the responsible party. In her book *The Purity Myth,* she says this about what she calls "the lie of virginity": "It's time to teach our daughters that their ability to be good people depends on their being good people, not on whether or not they are sexually active."[2]

She goes on to say: "It's high time to do away with outdated—and dangerous—notions of virginity. If young women's only ethical gauge is based on whether they're chaste, we're ensuring that they will continue to define themselves by their sexuality."[3] Valenti is right to some degree. Like second-wave feminists before her, she rightly asserts that women should not find their identity in sexuality, virginity, or anything else. But in her quest to rescue women from the so-called "purity myth," she makes morality fluid.

In her book, *Full Frontal Feminism: A Young Woman's Guide to Why Feminism Matters,* Valenti says that feminism says you own your sexuality. No one else can shame you for what you do with your body. She writes, "Feminism tells you it's okay to make decisions about your sexuality *for yourself*. Because when it comes down to it, what's more powerful and important than being able to do what you want with your body without fear of being shamed or punished?"[4]

The Modesty Wars

It's true that many Christians also argue that heralding purity as a biblical quality places undue pressure on women, and sometimes they've argued this point for good reason. Purity, modesty, and abstinence are not only a woman's problem. For those who profess godliness, they are everyone's challenge. The Bible leaves no person untouched in its standards for holiness and purity; God commands everyone to be holy because he is holy (Lev. 20:26).

If we are honest, the whole modesty debate can be more than a little divisive. Maybe you have been hurt by someone's criticism of your choice of clothing. You think, *My body is my own, right? Isn't it unfair for someone else to impose her standards about skirt length, pant tightness, and bathing suit choices on me?* Or maybe you think modesty is strictly a man's problem. If men would control their sexual impulses to lust, then women could dress however they like.

Right after I graduated from college, I lived in a house with four other girls. It was one of the best times of my life. Whenever one of us would prepare to leave the house, we would state the popular mantra "modest is hottest" to each other, implying that proper coverage was the key to a man's heart and attraction to us. Of course, we were joking. Most of my roommates grew up in a conservative Christian subculture that praised covering up and reviled the opposite. So we were all navigating our way through what pleased God regarding our clothes. I learned a lot from my roommates in those years.

Because God saved me out of a hypersexualized lifestyle, my quest for modesty often led me toward legalism. I knew what it was to entice the eyes of men to lust after me, so I was terrified of falling back into the same sin. I was reluctant to show my body in *any* way, even if what I wore would be considered modest by the most conservative among us. My roommates provided me a helpful place to process those emotions and fears. We all were coming from less than biblical backgrounds.

Modesty in the Shadow of the Fall

Within the Christian subculture, the pendulum has swung to both ends of the modesty spectrum over the years. Some have said that the current modesty talk is actually causing women to feel shame over their bodies, when in fact God made the female body beautiful.[5] Is this perception accurate?

The Bible never presents modesty as a covering for the shame of a woman's body. God created men and women in his image, and this means he created a woman's body for his glory. The Song of Solomon, written by a man who is very attracted to his future wife's body, is full of vivid imagery. God created a woman's body to be visually appealing to a man, but not just any man. Within the beautiful love story of Song of Solomon we find these careful words: "Do not awaken love before its appropriate time" (2:7; 3:5; 8:4 HCSB). There is a time and place for enjoying the wife of your youth. God never presents a woman's body as shameful, distasteful, or something to keep hidden, but he does give parameters for how we are to view it.

Any discussion of modesty and purity (or simply life in general) must carry with it an understanding of what it means to live in this fallen world. It is true that our bodies are temples of the Holy Spirit (1 Cor. 6:19). It is also true that our bodies bring glory to God (v. 20). But part of that glory is only meant to be seen and experienced within the covenant of marriage. Adam and Eve were naked and unashamed precisely because of the covenant (Gen. 2:25). It was only when, and immediately after, the covenant was marred by sin that they frantically tried to cover their nakedness (3:7).

As I was preparing to get married, the dress shop owner where I bought my wedding dress recounted how she had just helped a high school student find a prom dress. The result, I was told, was that the girl looked amazing in her prom dress. She had chosen a tight, strapless minidress for the event, and the owner remarked that this girl had "a body to die for." In her mind, the girl had it, and she deserved to flaunt it. Tragically, this is our culture's common response to a woman's body. Beauty is defined by our sexuality. The notion of covering up or reserving your body for one man sounds like a foreign language to our culture of excess and sexual aggression. What the shop owner was saying was classic third-wave feminism language, whether she knew it or not. If a woman has an attractive figure, then it only seems right that she show off the assets she has been afforded. It makes less sense in the eyes of our culture to cover up. And it is even more unheard of to allow someone else to make that decision for you. Modesty to our culture is seen as embarrassment over what we have been given, namely our bodies. But to God modesty is actually respecting what we have been given and protecting what God has deemed private and not for public consumption. The culture links beauty with sexuality, flaunting your body with freedom. These are all distortions of true beauty.

For Christians, covering up is not about shame or embarrassment over our bodies. God is not ashamed of our bodies. He created us. But we live in a post-Genesis 3 world, where we are no longer "naked and unashamed." Every morning when we put on clothing, it is a reminder that things are not as they should be. We can't go back to the perfection of Eden, and many displays of our body are not glorifying to God simply because they reveal what God has seen fit to cover.

John Piper has this to say about modesty in the shadow of the fall:

> You are not what you were and you are not what you ought to be. The chasm between what you are and what you ought to be is huge. Covering yourself with clothing is a right response to this—not to conceal it, but to confess it. Henceforth, you shall wear clothing, not to conceal that you are not what you should be, but to confess that you are not what you should be. One practical implication of this is that public nudity today is not a return to innocence but rebellion against moral reality. God ordains clothes to witness to the glory we have lost, and it is added rebellion to throw them off.[6]

Our discussions surrounding modesty must consider that *God* clothes Adam and Eve (Gen. 3:21). He saw fit to cover their nakedness, not because he was ashamed of their bodies, but because part of their glory had been lost when they sinned. Like everything around us, things are not as they were intended to be. Modesty is more than simply covering up certain body parts. It is a declaration that this world is not all God intended it to be. God is the one who clothes us, and makes us modest.

Modesty matters precisely because we live in a post-Genesis 3 world. Everyone is telling a story about their relationship to God by what they choose to wear (or not to wear).

Purity in an Impure World

Just like modesty is a hot (or unpopular) topic in our culture, purity is equally divisive. You probably hear it all the time from teachers, parents, pastors, friends—purity is important. God wants you to stay pure. Don't have sex until you are married. Maybe you made a purity pledge and wore a ring to symbolize your commitment. Or maybe you live a double life, acting like you follow the purity commitment while secretly going against what you say you believe. Maybe you just don't care. You have heard all of this before, and think the purity path is a really boring and outdated way to live.

But like modesty, purity also is God's idea. Therefore, any understanding of purity must first begin with a right understanding of God. We are to be holy because God is holy. God is pure, holy, and good. If we are in Christ, and children of God, we should want nothing less than what he himself already is. Christians do not see purity as a burden but as a joy (Ps. 51:10; Matt. 5:8).

The problem is that so many of us want to know how far we can go. We want to know how much is too much. Where's the line and how close can I get to it? We are faced with a dilemma. We want the attention of the world, but not too much. We want the bell to ring for us, but we're offended when it does. We ask those questions because we are pulled by the world's understanding of sex and beauty. It seems fun. It seems adventurous and freeing. But God never takes us there. He gives us one simple command: "I am holy, and if you are my people, you are to be holy like me." But what is our problem with that command? So many of us try to be holy on our own; we try on our own to fit into God's standards for morality, only to be crushed by those standards time and time again. We can't do the very thing he commands us to do. How many times have you thought, I am not going to cuss anymore. I am not going to watch those kinds of movies again. I am not going to lie anymore. I am not going to have sex with that guy, or send a sexual text message, or flirt with the guys at school or work. I'm not going to fantasize about the man I saw at the store. How many times have you sinned and woken up the next day feeling like a failure because you just can't stop doing it? I know I have thought those same regretful thoughts. We hear the command that sexual immorality must not even be "named" among us (Eph. 5:3), and we shudder at what impure thoughts come across our minds. To understand what it means to be pure and holy, we must understand God. And to understand God we need Jesus to cleanse us from our sin. If we are truly honest, our lives often are Romans 7 on display. The good we want to do we don't, and vice versa.

Purity is not a list of rules to be followed. It is not a ring to be worn or a card to be signed. It is a lifestyle (Titus 2:4–5). It is a lifestyle of a person who has been bought with Christ's blood and loves God the Father. It is a lifestyle of war, where we daily flee from sin (1 Cor. 6:18). God is not pleased with a "cleaned-up act." The Bible tells us that even our good deeds are like filthy rags to God because we have been stained by sin (Isa. 64:6).

God's Design for Sex

Once we have a right understanding of God, we need to then understand how God created us. God created us as sexual beings. Sex was his idea. In Genesis 2:18–24 we see that God created Eve for Adam, and they were one flesh. It was not good for Adam to be alone, the text tells us. God created them distinctly different, and he created them for each other. But unfortunately sin marred what God created to be good. Sex is distorted, and the result is a world now filled with all forms of perversions of what God designed sex to be. Third-wave feminism says that we get to define sex. Sex is for us and about us. Our impulses and our pleasures rule us. But that is not what God says.

God designed women to desire intimacy with a man. Part of being human is having sexual desires. We do not check them at the door when we become Christians. Consider, for example, the woman in Song of Solomon, who was eager to have sex with her future husband (Song 1:2; 2:3, 5; 4:16; 5:16; 7:11; 8:14). But God has given us parameters for his good gift of sex. We can enjoy his gift fully, but we can also make his gift a destructive force in our lives. This gift is only to be experienced within the bounds of a marriage between one man and one woman. Anything outside of these boundaries is outside of God's design. And if God is calling you to be married some day, then any sexual experience with someone else before your wedding day is outside of God's design as well. God wants you to be holy because he is holy. He loves you and wants what is best for you.

In Song of Solomon, the married woman urges the single women around her to not arouse her desires until it is time. Throughout the entire book she pleads with the young maidens to abstain from awakening desires that are not ready to be awakened. It is not simply about "having sex." It is about giving yourself over to the desires that are intended only for your future husband. There is the right timing for this gift. Just because God gave you desires does not mean you get to act on them. The entire Christian life is about waiting and patience. We are not free to do as we please. Tim Keller has this to say about God's design for sex:

> To call the marriage "one flesh," then, means that sex is understood as both a sign of that personal, legal union and a means to accomplish it. The Bible says don't unite with someone physically unless you are also willing to unite with the person emotionally, personally, socially, economically, and legally. Don't become physically naked and vulnerable to the other person without becoming vulnerable in every other way, because you have given up your freedom and bound yourself in marriage.
>
> Then, once you have given yourself in marriage, sex is a way of maintaining and deepening that union as the years go by. . . . Indeed, sex is perhaps the most powerful God-created way to help you give your entire self to another human being. Sex is God's appointed way for two people to reciprocally say to one another "I belong completely, permanently, and exclusively to you." You must not use sex to say anything less.[7]

Isn't that the exact opposite of how our culture defines sex and marriage? Sex in our culture is shown to be most freeing, most exhilarating, and most enjoyable outside of marriage, not within it.

In light of the fact that we are to be holy because God is holy, and in light of the fact that sex is a good thing, how are we supposed to live?

Let's get some help from the book of Proverbs. Proverbs is an Old Testament book of wisdom, and many of the proverbs were written by King Solomon for his son. Throughout the book, we frequently see him pleading with his son to listen to his words. He has experienced the effects of sin. He knows what he is talking about. And he has wisdom for us today in how to live as pure women. Proverbs 5–7 is a plea to flee sexual immorality. Solomon is begging with his son to run from the forbidden woman.

This woman's life leads to death and destruction for all who come in contact with her (Prov. 5:1–14). But what is she doing? She is a woman who is set on leading men into adultery. She uses her sexuality to lure men away from their wives and their purity.

The Forbidden Woman versus Lady Wisdom

The contrast between the woman of Proverbs 7 and the woman of wisdom in the book of Proverbs is striking. If we are going to live as biblical women in a feminist world, we should pay careful attention to Solomon's words about a woman who walks in wisdom and the cautions he provides about the woman who doesn't. It's not hard to see that some things never change, even many centuries later. Notice five characteristics about this "forbidden woman."

1. She is dressed as a prostitute (Prov. 7:10). Her clothing communicates that she is sexually available to men. Modesty is not simply about covering up your body; it is about a desire for attention. Women are tempted by the lust to be lusted after. We want the bell to ring for us. But outside of marriage, any man's desire for us is sinful.

2. She makes herself available to everyone (Prov. 7:11–12). She goes to the streets, the market, and anywhere she knows men will be. She is loud and makes herself known. Are you this type of woman? Do you make yourself available to every guy who comes in contact with you? Do you call, text, and flirt with the guys in your school, church, or workplace? Faithfulness to one man begins before you say "I do" and continues until one of you takes that final breath.
3. Not only does she make herself available, she also uses her immodesty and availability to lure men to her (Prov. 7:13–18, 21). She is thinking only about her own temporary pleasure and gain.
4. She is married and using her husband's time away as an opportunity to commit adultery (Prov. 7:19–20). No matter what your circumstance right now, if you are impure with a man who is not your husband—even if it is your boyfriend and you say you love him—you are living like the forbidden woman. The reality is that if he is not your husband right now, he very well could be someone else's husband someday—and you could be someone else's future wife. Even if you do end up marrying him someday, you have awakened desire "before its appropriate time." You are operating outside of God's good design, therefore it is sin. And if you are married, you are just as susceptible to the forces of attraction as those who are single. If you are not careful to protect your emotions and thoughts, you could very easily slip into temptation to turn from your husband and lust after another man.
5. Her actions lead men into death (Prov. 7:22–23). Succumbing to lust can cost a man his life, and it can cost a woman her life as well. Impurity today might not lead to your immediate physical death, but it will ultimately be your destruction.

Those in Christ should not desire to be like the forbidden woman—even if all you see around you are women who live this way. Thankfully, God is kind to tell us how to live pure lives as women. Proverbs repeatedly talks about Lady Wisdom and encourages the believer in Jesus to follow her example. If you want to be a woman of wisdom, consider these examples.

1. Lady Wisdom's beauty is inward, not outward (Prov. 31:30). It's not wrong to want to look attractive. But a woman's clothing should not be her primary focus (1 Pet. 3:3–4). We should not dress to make ourselves the primary attraction. Christian women should desire to make Christ the main attraction. When we dress immodestly, we take away from Christ's glory. By being lusted after, we are getting glory and attention for ourselves, not the One who made us.

   I enjoy shopping, and I enjoy doing my hair and makeup in the morning. I don't like going out without makeup on, although now that I have young kids I sometimes forego makeup for the sake of ease. I try to pay attention to the latest fashions. These things are not wrong in themselves. But if I leave my house thinking, *I hope everyone loves my outfit. I hope that person notices me*, then I have misplaced desires. Remember my story about being a waitress? I shouldn't want anyone other than my husband ringing a bell for me. My body is not an object of affection for everyone in Little Rock—and neither is yours for your town. One practical way that we can love our brothers in Christ (and all men) is to be mindful of what we wear. Men are visually stimulated. They are designed to want to look at a woman's body. And we are designed to want them to. But our bodies are only for one man in the covenant of marriage.
2. Lady Wisdom makes herself available to one man (Prov. 31:23, 28). God never intended for us to be serial daters. The Bible does not give us a framework for the dating culture that we have today. We were made to enjoy intimacy, both emotional and physical, with one man—our husband. In Genesis 2, we see that Eve was made for Adam. She was made to complete him. Flirting and tempting guys with your affections and your body opens doors for intimacy with them.
3. Lady Wisdom is faithful (Prov. 31:11–12). Godly women know that engaging in any sexual activity with a man before marriage

is committing adultery against her future husband. Jesus says in Matthew 5:28 that if one has even looked at a woman lustfully, he has committed adultery. And if you tempt a man to lust after you, whether by your physical actions with him or your physical appearance, you have tempted him to commit adultery. It is important to note that it takes two people to lust in this situation—the person lusting and the one causing the lusting. Men are not off the hook for their lustful thoughts, but as a woman you can help them in this battle by dressing in a way that honors God and them. And if you look lustfully at a guy, or a girl, you have committed the same sin. The godly woman knows that God's Word is true and that marriage to one man is the only faithful way to express sexuality.

4. Lady Wisdom is life-giving (Prov. 31:13–16, 18–20, 27). In Genesis 3:20, Adam names his wife *Eve* as the "mother of all living." As we've already talked about, women are given the task of being life-givers. We are to bear and nurture life in all settings, no matter our age. The forbidden woman's life leads to death for all who come in contact with her. But the godly woman labors hard to cultivate life in the people around her. Do not be a source of death for the brothers in your life. Encourage them in their walk with the Lord and their fight against lust by your appearance, your actions, and your relationship with them.

If you have failed in any of these areas, there is hope! The impurity of today does not need to be the final word in your life. If you find yourself broken over your sexual immorality, a fountain of grace is available for you at the cross of Christ. He was destroyed so you don't have to be if you simply trust him through repentance and faith.

True Beauty

We live in a culture that is obsessed with image, and every day advertisements bombard us with promises to deliver beauty and happiness. Many of us struggle to leave the house content because of the constant anxiety we feel over looking "beautiful enough." With all of the hype surrounding being beautiful, we must ask ourselves, What exactly is beauty? Every day we are faced with a choice: Will we choose worldly beauty, defined by fashion magazines and the culture? Or will we choose godly beauty, defined by the perfect, holy words of our God?

As Christians, we can have a love/hate relationship with beauty. We want to guard against worldliness, so we minimize beauty. Or we swing too far the other way and think it doesn't matter how we think about beauty. But the Bible is not silent on the subject of beauty. And if we are going to make any headway in recovering from the influences of feminism, we must learn what God has to say about beauty and our bodies.

In their book, *True Beauty,* Carolyn Mahaney and Nicole Whitacre define beauty in this way: "True beauty is to behold and reflect the beauty of God."[8]

They go on to say that God is the author of beauty and he is the truly beautiful one. By creating us in his image, he gave us his beauty. When we behold him, the one who made us and loves us, we are reflecting his beauty.

Because we were created in God's image, we were made to desire and notice beauty. When we see a precious new baby or a beautiful man or woman, we acknowledge such beauty because God is the Creator of these things. The entire book of Song of Solomon is full of references to both the man and the woman's praise of the beauty of the other. The biblical authors even made mention of beautiful people like Sarah (Gen. 12:11), Rachel (Gen. 29:17), Joseph (Gen. 39:6), David (1 Sam. 16:12), Absalom (2 Sam. 14:25), the woman who tended to King David before he died (1 Kings 1:4), and Esther (Est. 2:7).

We know that there were beautiful women in the Bible. And we know that God is the author of beauty. But it's critical to remember that outward beauty is not everything. Being beautiful is not a sin, but, for example, if Esther had sought her own gain and refused to help her people, her beauty would have meant nothing. And though Sarah was beautiful, she probably would have traded her beauty for a baby. Absalom's beauty led to pride, and his downfall (2 Sam. 18:9–15). And Joseph's beauty landed him in jail, falsely accused (Gen. 39:1–23).

Everything around us is a reminder that we cannot trust in external beauty. All of us are subject to the natural process of aging. And even in our youthfulness, we could all probably confess that many times our daily date with the mirror leaves much to be desired.

There is no arguing that women want to be beautiful. Beauty is a gift, and I will be the first to admit that I want to be beautiful just as much as the next girl. But I also must recognize that if my hope is in my designer hair straightener and my Great Lash mascara, I will end up disappointed and discontent. There is a healthy balance between being feminine and making the products of femininity an idol.

When you and I walk out of our homes, we face a barrage of self-criticism and comparison to others around us. And it's easy when we walk into a group of women for our first reaction to be judging the beauty of those around us, even to the point of gossip: "Did you see what she was wearing?" We must repent of such things.

Unless we see that all of our comparisons and self-criticisms are fundamentally prideful and that they express unbelief in God, we will spend our entire lives never feeling good enough—and that is a worldview that will ultimately lead us to death. When women bury themselves in a sea of credit card debt just to buy the newest designer style, they are at their core saying, "God is not really God. The praise of others is." Hugging a cold toilet after forcing oneself to throw up is fundamentally saying, "God does not meet my needs, and he is not sovereign over my weight." Obsession with image, no matter how detrimental it is to your health or well-being, is a form of pride and self-worship—just like all of our disbelief is pride and self-worship.

We can, and should, recognize beautiful, modest, godly women when we see them. But we should not hope in those affirmations in our own life. Our mood should not rise or fall with compliments about our dress or new shoes. And, most importantly, our characterization of beauty must not come from the latest issue of *InStyle* magazine.

If the Lord allows us to live until we are eighty years old, few will remember the face of our 20s, 30s, or 40s. All they will see is the wrinkled face of a woman nearing the end of her life. As we prepare to meet our Savior, no amount of Botox or fad diet will prepare us for our final breath. Only a life spent pouring over the mirror of God's Word will prepare us for that glorious day.

It's easy to pay lip service to the truths of the Bible, yet still live in constant anxiety and unbelief. The fight of faith is hard. If you feel yourself struggling with true beauty versus worldly beauty, ask God to reveal the areas in your life that need to be changed. Preach the gospel to yourself daily. If you find yourself anxious about how you look in the morning, proclaim Christ to your wayward heart. Do not choose bondage to the world's ideals any longer—choose life in Christ. Let us not be ashamed to recognize true beauty when we see it, but put our hope in Jesus's blood and righteousness, lest we think on that final day that it's our trendy outfits and size 2 bodies that will save us.

Beauty Points to the Creator

God has created every inch of the universe, every cloud in the sky, and every hair on your head. Your understanding of beauty must first be rooted in a proper theology of God. If God created all things, then the created things should reflect the Creator—God himself. And if beauty is truth, then all things, to be truly beautiful, must point to the ultimate truth—God, himself.[9]

Beauty is defined by the One who created beauty. Do you purchase new shoes, or get your hair cut, or buy makeup to put Christ on display, or for man's empty praise?

Some Christians might think that beauty is something to be avoided. But if God created the earth and saw that it was very good (Gen. 1:31), then we must believe that he didn't create it ugly and call it good. Why are we drawn to things that are attractive, if God does not want things to be beautiful? It is our fallen nature that distorts true beauty. God created us with a desire for things beautiful because he wants us to worship him. When we divorce beauty from God, we live in an endless cycle of trying to meet the newest standard of beauty, from plastic surgery to cosmetics that promise to make us look years younger and have flawless skin. Beauty becomes about us, rather than the Creator—and it is never enough.

So how does this affect our relationship with the mirror and closet? If your shirt is drawing more attention to body parts than your person, you are not declaring the beauty and truth of Christ. If you want your outfit to draw more attention to your impeccable style than your heart for Jesus, it is not declaring true beauty. We should want to be beautiful, but not so we can win pageant awards, a host of boyfriends, or the compliments of our friends. We should want to be beautiful because we want people to see our Christ.

Peter addressed this in 1 Peter 3:3: "Do not let your adornment be external—the braiding of hair, and the putting on of gold jewelry, or the clothing you wear." As Mahaney and Whitacre said, true beauty is beholding and reflecting God, which is what Peter is getting at. Our lives should be about worshiping God in everything and pointing back to him in all we do. As I said in chapter 3, this hidden beauty is a gentle and quiet spirit—a resolute hope in the God who holds our life together. This is how we reflect inner beauty.

Now surely Peter is not telling us to forego clothing. He isn't. Rather, he is saying that our outward appearance should not define us, and most certainly it should not be a distraction in worship and daily living. There is much freedom in Christ regarding makeup use, hairstyles, and clothing. But all of these things should seek a common purpose—displaying the glory of Christ. Christians, of all people, should be the most beauty-seeking people in society because we know the real source and definition of beauty.

The heavens are not silent—they are declaring the glory of God (Ps. 19:1). Is your appearance declaring the same thing? Do you seek to point people to Jesus, or to your newest dress? May your lives and appearance declare the same thing—Jesus Christ is Lord, to the glory of God the Father.

Finding Pleasure in God Alone

Perhaps you don't see a problem with your impurity. You are happy to continue with your life of sexual immorality because you don't really see anything wrong with it. You enjoy the pleasure and attention it affords you. You like the clothes you wear and feel empowered when you leave the house. But is it really satisfying you? If you were honest with yourself, would you be able to say that it is enough? The reason why you go back to your boyfriend, or back to self-pleasing, or back to flirting is because you can't get enough. Third-wave feminism promises that your body is your own and you can do whatever you like with it, consequence free. But the Bible tells a different story. You were designed to receive maximum fulfillment in Jesus only, and the very fact that you keep going back to your sin even though you feel unsatisfied in the morning is because you are trying to make those acts mean something they were never designed to mean. There is a void in your soul that only Jesus can fill. No person on earth can fill that for you.

Or maybe your life feels fine the way it is because you don't ever do anything that bad. But have you ever lusted and wished you could act on it? If you haven't, praise God for that. The only reason you are still standing pure to this day is by the grace and mercy of Jesus Christ. Ask him to continue giving you grace.

Perhaps you feel broken over your sin. You feel like there is no hope for a sinner like you. You know what it feels like to desperately want attention and do anything to get it. You know what it feels like to wake up in the morning and feel miserable over your actions the previous night but you just don't know where to turn. I encourage you, dear sister, that there is a fountain of grace for you at the cross of Jesus Christ. The Bible says that he is living water (John 4:10–11). He is life. He is salvation for those who turn from their sin and trust in his death and resurrection alone (Acts 4:12). Do not despair. There is no sin so great that he is not sufficient to conquer with his finished work (1 Cor. 6:9–11).

The point of purity is not just to make it to marriage without having sex. It's not about getting to marriage and doing whatever you want after you say, "I do." It's about God and obeying him because we love him. You were not made for sexual immorality; you were made for God (1 Cor. 6:13–20). Purity and modesty are lifelong pursuits. All our attempts at purity without the shed blood of Jesus on our behalf are worthless. We need him in our fight to stay pure. I am married, and I still need him daily to fight my sinful tendency toward impurity. All these years later, I still feel that pull from the restaurant—in my flesh I want that bell to ring loudly.

God cares about your heart. He cares about your soul. He cares about what you worship. He wants you to worship him only—not sex, not men, not popularity, not work, not beauty, not fun, not friends, not even church. Purity is important because the Creator of the universe, and of you, is pure. Purity is important because his Son, Jesus Christ, was the purest man who ever lived. And he died to make us pure. He died to cleanse us from our impurity. The sad reality is that even if you have never engaged in any sexual immorality—you are still an impure person in need of Christ's purity. We all are. But the great hope is that we can have Jesus. Do not look to your own attempts at purity. They will fail you every time. Instead, look to Jesus; he is the hope for impure people like you and me.

Restoration in My Life

Feminism tells us that our bodies are our own to use how we please. But God tells us otherwise. As image bearers, we are to display his glory to a watching world. We are not our own; we are created beings meant to point to the Creator.

For the Single Woman

Inventory your closet. Based on the biblical standards for purity and the fact that your body is not your own, are there any pieces in your closet that tell a different story than the one you were intended to tell with your body? Do you struggle with wanting the bell to ring for you? If so, this is a two-fold problem. One, you want the attention of many, rather than the one God has for you. Two, you are treating your body as your own to display, rather than a gift given to you by God. Ask God to give you a heart of faithfulness to his standards for beauty and purity and a fresh perspective on your body being his and not your own.

For the Married Woman

It's easy to think that you can take a big sigh of relief regarding purity once you say, "I do." I know I did. But as I got into the daily grind of my marriage, I realized that vigilance regarding purity and holiness was just as important this side of the nuptials. The stakes are high in marriage and out of marriage. Do you take liberties with what you allow into your mind through movies, television shows, magazines, and conversations because you think it doesn't impact you now that you are married? Do you dress immodestly because you or your husband like showing off your body you have worked hard for? Ask God for wisdom and unity for both you and your husband as you seek to honor the Lord and his standards for your body.

Study Questions

1. What comes to your mind when you hear the words *modesty* and *purity*? Do you have a negative or a positive reaction to the words? How does your reaction compare to the definitions in this chapter

of purity and modesty? (*Purity:* a lifestyle of a person who has been bought by Christ's blood and who loves her holy God. *Modesty:* a daily declaration that this world is not what God intended, by covering what God saw fit to cover in the garden.)

2. How do you see the culture impacting your own understanding of beauty and purity?

3. If you feel comfortable, share some of your practical application points from the "Restoration in My Life" section.

5

God's Design for the Home

Some years ago, I was sitting in a conference breakout session with a group of twenty-something women at a Christian college. Like many of the women in the room, I was young, eager to get married, and hoping to learn more about how to grow as a woman. The conference focused on passionate commitment to Christ, and while I don't remember the exact details of the breakout session, I know it was geared toward how we could apply that passion to our lives as women.

During the question and answer time following the session, one girl timidly relayed her dilemma to the speaker: "Whenever people ask me at school what I want to be when I graduate, I have a hard time knowing what to say. I really want to be a wife and mom. Is it wrong if I just say that?"

She went on to share that she felt like her response was lackluster, and met with awkward remarks and blank stares. She wanted encouragement that her desires for her life weren't as strange as the world around her made them out to be.

The speaker offered a little encouragement, but primarily was at a loss for words. She had just finished giving a talk on calling and ministry. She had just finished spurring on the next generation to get involved in leadership. I imagine she wasn't expecting a young woman to stand up and say, "I really want to be a wife and mom."

She's not the only one.

At the time, I was growing in my desire to embrace marriage and motherhood, and I lived with other Christian women who felt the same. Sure, we were single and working nine-to-five jobs, but deep down many of us wanted to be married with a sweet baby on our hip. While the speaker, to her credit, was affirmative of the young woman's desire to be a stay-at-home wife and mother, her confusion over the question shows just how far we have shifted in the choices women have.

Betty Friedan and the proponents of second-wave feminism launched women out of the home and into the workforce. Friedan critiqued the 1950s and 1960s housewife who doted on her children and played bridge with her lady friends. Women want something more, Friedan said. Women don't want to be *just* housewives or *just* moms. They have gifts and abilities that deserve to be used broadly, in various contexts and settings.

Fast forward fifty years, and women now have more choices than ever. A woman doesn't have to be "just a housewife" if she doesn't want to be. But then again, if a woman chooses to define herself as "just a wife and mom," even if she is a successful attorney and the First Lady of the United States, she is praised for her choice. Maybe you remember the 2008 presidential election. In her speech at the Democratic National Convention, Michelle Obama defined herself not as the accomplished attorney that she was (and is), but as a wife, mom, daughter, and sister.[1] Some viewed this as a step backward for women, saying that women should not be defined only by their relationships to others, particularly men. But others viewed this is a step forward. We live in a time where a powerful woman, like Mrs. Obama, can define herself any way she chooses and still retain her identity.

We've come a long way since Friedan's day. But women are still in a battle regarding the home and our place in it.

In a 2003 *New York Times Magazine* piece, Lisa Belkin chronicled the lives of elite, working mothers who chose to leave prestigious careers in order to stay home with their children. Much to the chagrin of feminists, these mothers changed the landscape of feminism—choosing motherhood over the corporate ladder.

> Arguably, the barriers of 40 years ago are down. Fifty percent of the undergraduate class of 2003 at Yale was female; this year's graduating class at Berkeley Law School was 63 percent women; Harvard was 46 percent; Columbia was 51. Nearly 47 percent of medical students are women, as are 50 percent of undergraduate business majors (though, interestingly, about 30 percent of M.B.A. candidates). They are recruited by top firms in all fields. They start strong out of the gate.
>
> And then, suddenly, they stop. Despite all those women graduating from law school, they comprise only 16 percent of partners in law firms. Although men and women enter corporate training programs in equal numbers, just 16 percent of corporate officers are women, and only eight companies in the Fortune 500 have female C.E.O.'s. Of 435 members of the House of Representatives, 62 are women; there are 14 women in the 100-member Senate.[2]

But many years later, it wasn't all fun and games for these women. *The New York Times* followed up with many of these mothers who were featured in this "Opt Out Revolution" story (they were also featured in news outlets like *60 Minutes* and *Time* magazine).[3] These mothers, who were so confident in their decision to trade in their lucrative careers for the daily grind of caring for their children, were facing an identity crisis. They, like the women of Friedan's era, were wondering if there was something more than playdates, peanut butter sandwiches, and craft time. They wondered if they had given up too much. They wondered if they were made for more than this.

What happened? Why did something that promised to fulfill come back void?

In some ways, the disillusionment these women experienced when they left their careers for the home comes from a cultural misunderstanding of work. In our society, work is something you get paid for. That leaves many stay-at-home moms, volunteers, and anyone who helps someone for no compensation left to wonder what she is doing all day long. In God's economy, work is something you do because you bear his image. God worked in bringing forth creation, and when he created man and woman in his image, he commanded them to do the same (Gen. 1:1–28). This means that whatever occupation we choose, we are all created to work. But there was also something more to their disenfranchisement with being stay-at-home moms—the perpetual problem of their identity.

The Problem of Identity

As we saw in chapter 1, when we find our identity in anything other than the image of God, we will inevitably face an identity crisis. In the 1950s, the pinnacle of a woman's life was her home. Her home was her domain and her identity. Betty Friedan saw something wrong with that and encouraged women out of the home and into a life of greater purpose. While her diagnosis of misplaced identity was correct, she simply replaced one idol for another. Now the workplace is the identity. What a woman accomplishes in society is what defines her. And now here we are in twenty-first-century America, and many women are trying to do it all. We are endlessly having the discussion about whether women can have a home life and a work life—and whether she can do everything with skill and ease. Frankly and understandably, I think a lot of women are just exhausted with it all.

The issue lies in the fact that these things were never meant to fulfill us. Motherhood, while good and life-changing, is not our identity. Our home, while important and necessary, is not our identity. Our career, while fulfilling and challenging, does not define us.

Our marital status, while enjoyable and rewarding, is not where we find our hope.

What feminism failed to answer was this question of identity. Where should a woman find her sense of self-worth? Where should she put her hope?

Our circumstances are always changing. When we place all of our eggs in the basket of motherhood, career, home, marital status, gifting, or some combination of all of these, we will *always* come up short. We can be stripped of those things at a moment's notice. Any understanding of our role in the home must first be rooted in the fact that our identity is never to be found there. It is to be found in Christ.

The Problem of Purpose

One of the common responses from these mothers of the "opt-out revolution" was that there were never enough things in the day to make them feel like they were doing something of value. No amount of volunteering, scrubbing the floor, or cooking nutritious meals ever gave them a sense of true purpose over the long haul. Betty Friedan got this too. The 1950s housewife was stifled, she said. She needed purpose and meaning that went beyond just keeping a nice home and making sure her husband was happy:

> If I am right, the problem that has no name stirring in the minds of so many American women today is not a matter of loss of femininity or too much education, or the demands of domesticity. It is far more important than anyone recognizes. It is the key to these other new and old problems which have been torturing women and their husbands and their children, and puzzling their doctors and educators for years. It may well be the key to our future as a nation and a culture. We can no longer ignore that voice within women that says: "I want something more than my husband and my children and my home."[4]

Friedan couldn't see beyond the children, husband, and home and recognize that there was purpose in that life of domesticity.

She only saw the work as menial and beneath all that women were capable of.

This is not foreign to us today either, even in Christian circles. The concept of the home is often maligned and easily misunderstood. In her 2012 book, *A Year of Biblical Womanhood,* Rachel Held Evans embarked on a task to try to live up to all of the Bible's commands to women. In her chapter on domesticity, she attempted a variety of "home oriented" tasks, including cooking through a Martha Stewart book, hosting a dinner party, and making Thanksgiving dinner. She wrote:

> The importance of homemaking in the contemporary biblical womanhood movement cannot be overstated, and proponents tend to use strong, unequivocal language to argue that the only sphere in which a woman can truly bring glory to God is the home.[5]

Before we get any further, I can assure you that you will not hear me say the above statement in this chapter, or anywhere else in this book. Homemaking is not the pinnacle of greatness for a woman. Biblical womanhood is not striving to make us all evangelical Martha Stewarts who make our meals from scratch and always have crisply folded bedsheets. Nor is the home the only place a woman can bring glory to God. But godly womanhood does not completely disregard the home either, though Martha Stewart or any of the "domestic divas" of our current culture are not godly models for us to follow. Not by a long shot. We have to recover a biblical understanding of our home and its purpose, and stop promoting the home and homemaking as a kind of twenty-first-century caricature of a celebrity. Sure, cooking, cleaning, and entertaining are important and can serve great purposes for God's glory—but that is exactly the point. They're about *God,* not about us.

If every facet of our lives is designed to bring glory to God, then surely the home has more value than mere cleanliness and gourmet meals. If, as God's image-bearers, we show God's character to a watching world through our womanhood, then even our home has value.

What Is the Home?

Most Christian women are familiar with Paul's exhortation to Titus that older women are to encourage younger women to be "working at home" (Titus 2:5). Over the years, interpretations of this verse have varied widely. I won't rehash all of them here. But they range from saying that a woman's only sphere of influence should be the home to treating this command as irrelevant for us today. I reject both of these extremes.

Before we begin talking about a woman's role in the home, we have to understand what exactly the home is. In *The Measure of Success: Uncovering the Biblical Perspective on Women, Work, and the Home,* authors Carolyn McCulley and Nora Shank provide a history of the home and how the consumerism and industry that began with the Industrial Revolution changed the home from being a place of productivity to a place of consumerism.

They say that for women like Katie Luther (wife of Martin Luther) and Sarah Edwards (wife of Jonathan Edwards), the work of the husband was the work of the whole family unit. The family all worked together to make their home a place of refuge, hospitality, and productivity. But when the Industrial Revolution arrived with all of its factories and increased work, the family unit began moving in a myriad of directions.

> When the American home became a showcase for consumption, it altered centuries of productivity and introduced a number of present challenges. First, the home had stopped being a place that generated income. Though it was good that new occupations had opened for women outside of the home, now they had to figure out how to rear a family and provide for themselves while working in different locations.

> Second, in the process of demeaning domesticity, the culture neglects to validate the significance of the work done in the home to care for others. The private sphere remains a place where unpaid work has eternal merit. In accepting the culture of consumerism, homes become a monument to personal style and taste, rather than places of service to others. These days the "new domesticity" popularized on blogs and social media sites is wildly popular; and it brings with it the same aspirations about productivity idealized in the glossy ads of the 1950s. It sells a lifestyle.[6]

The purpose of the home, McCulley and Shank say, is not to showcase all of your nice things and reveal that you have arrived as a domestic goddess. The purpose of the home is about "feeding souls, providing a refuge for the weary, and living generously."[7] The home is a place of work. It's a place where life happens. It's a place where the family works together to accomplish God's purposes.

When I was first married, I felt pressured to live up to the expectations of Martha Stewart and the Food Network. I wanted to have a nice home (an apartment in my case). I wanted to have pretty centerpieces. I wanted the bathroom to always be tidy. And when we had people over, I wanted to impress them with my culinary skills. On our first weekend home from our honeymoon, I went grocery shopping on a Saturday afternoon. My excitement over my perfectly planned meal for the evening quickly waned when I got lost on the way to the grocery store. My plans were ruined. Not only did it take me all afternoon to even find the grocery store, but I lost valuable time that I needed to complete my perfectly planned-out homemade meal. Over the course of our first few weeks of marriage, I repeatedly felt like I was failing in this whole home thing. I worked full time outside of the home, and I couldn't keep up with all of the things I thought would make me the perfect wife.

One day, as my husband and I were riding in the car together, he stopped me midsentence: "Court, I don't want you to feel like you have to make gourmet meals all of the time. I know you feel this pressure to make everything from scratch, but sometimes a frozen pizza is perfectly fine."

In fact, it was more than fine. It was great! My husband likes frozen pizza. He likes having a happy wife, too. And what he saw in those early weeks of marriage was that I was putting the tasks of the home above the purpose of the home. The purpose of the home is to be a place of refuge, grace, and productivity—not a platform for me to prove what a great homemaker I am. God is to get the glory in our homes. I was trying to do it all—and look like I had it all together. I felt the pressure to have a perfect home, yet also succeed in my work. I wanted my life to look like the magazine, not the laundry war zone it had become. I was putting tasks before purpose.

The Home: A Place of Hospitality

While Paul encourages wives to be busy at home, the Bible spends a lot more time talking about the importance of hospitality than it does the home itself. The home is meant to be used—and not just for our own leisure and rest.

Often when we talk about hospitality, we get a June Cleaver image in our minds: perfect dress, baked cookies always ready for guests, apron on and ready for cooking, and—of course—a spotless home. These images are not wrong in and of themselves, but they don't give the full biblical picture of hospitality, nor are they very realistic. These ideas of hospitality are merely external, and to view hospitality in this way can quickly make the woman who doesn't measure up feel inadequate and incapable of obeying God's command to be hospitable to one another. The truth is, all believers are called to live hospitable lives. Romans 12:13 tell us to "seek to show hospitality." Hospitality is a mark of a faithful believer to welcome others into your life. Much more could be said, but here are four key things that mark hospitality and should mark our homes.

1. Hospitality is a gospel issue. It is tempting to take a verse

like Romans 12:13 and simply obey it for obedience's sake. But the gospel truths Paul presents throughout the whole book of Romans, particularly chapters 1–11, set us up to hear what God would have for us by the time we get to Romans 12:13. Romans 1–11 is full of rich theological truths about what Christ has accomplished on our behalf. Romans 12–16 then teaches us how we ought to live out these truths. Paul first sets us up theologically so we can rightly engage in the practical tasks of the Christian life. The tasks don't make sense without the theological foundation. This is why, in 12:1, he urges them "by the mercies of God." With God's mercy in plain view in the previous chapters, Paul essentially says, *in light of all that you have learned about God's abundant grace and mercy toward you, here is how you live.* These truths apply to all who are in Christ.

To practice hospitality is to live out of a life changed by the gospel. Christ's amazing work is what people should see in us when we love them and minister to them.

2. Hospitality is an exercise in humility. To minister to people often means (and requires) that we die to our own desires. If you read all of Romans 12, you find many commands that pertain to selfless living. In verse 3, Paul tells us not to think more highly of ourselves than we ought to. In verse 10, he tells us to outdo each other in honor. We know that the ministry of hospitality often requires us to step outside of what is comfortable for the good of someone else. There is no room for pride when we minister to people through hospitality. Pride will hinder others from seeing Jesus, which is our ultimate aim. And giving people our time, love, and resources will destroy us and drain us if we are motivated by our own desires and wants.

3. Hospitality is not gender specific. I have heard it said many times that hospitality is a woman's job, but Paul makes it clear that this isn't the case—and we know from other passages of Scripture that Paul is not afraid to distinguish between the different callings on men and women. He doesn't make gender distinctions in

the command to show hospitality. In Titus 1:8, for example, we see that for a man to be qualified to lead God's people, he must be hospitable (among other things). Throughout the Gospels we encounter men (and women) who willingly invite Jesus and his disciples into their homes. The Bible shows us that God did not limit hospitality to a specific gender when he inspired Paul to pen these words.

4. Hospitality is not contingent on marital status. Along with thinking that hospitality is only for women, we also tend to associate hospitality with married women—especially those with their own homes and nice, new things. I have known single women who refrain from hospitality because they think they don't have enough space or own the right stuff. But once again, Paul does not make this distinction. If we believe that practicing hospitality is an opportunity to show the love of Christ to people, then surely this applies to single women (and men) too. Carolyn McCulley, a single woman, has an entire chapter on hospitality as a ministry in her book *Did I Kiss Marriage Goodbye?* She says that "our ministry through our homes is so important that women are included in all of the four major 'hospitality commands' in the New Testament."[8]

Perhaps you have a demanding job and are not home often; ask God to give you wisdom to live out this command in the midst of a hectic schedule. It might mean inviting over one guest a month. Maybe you are a mother of young children and are spent at the end of the day. For you, showing hospitality might mean inviting an unbelieving mom over to befriend her and to have your kids play together. God cares about a heart that desires to minister, not duty for duty's sake. Hospitality is not about serving a three-course meal or a chocolate cake made from scratch, though those are not bad things. Hospitality is about so much more than what you do. It's about an attitude of welcome—a heart that embraces others regardless of your circumstances.

One of the clearest pictures of biblical hospitality came to me when I least expected it. My husband and I took a trip to Nashville to celebrate our first wedding anniversary. While there, we attended the church of a pastor and pastor's wife whom we knew. After the service we visited with the wife and planned to be on our way, when out of the blue she said, "Why don't you come to our house for lunch?" We were honored. We knew they had company all weekend and were most likely exhausted from a Sunday ministering to others, but she insisted. I rode with her to her home, while my husband rode with her husband. She asked me how married life had been and encouraged me through her own story of being married for longer than I had been alive. When we arrived at her house, she asked me if I minded leftovers, and I helped her piece together lunch from the various meals they had over the weekend. We put together a quick dessert, and lunch was served. What stood out was not that we had leftovers or that it was spontaneous. What stood out was how freely they welcomed us into their home. To this day it is one of our favorite memories of our married life. This couple served us not only by providing us with a meal, but also by opening their lives and years of marital wisdom to a young couple who were just getting started and had a lot to learn.

We have been invited into God's family. He extended hospitality to us, and this should make us grateful. The desire to be hospitable should come out of the overflow of a humble heart changed by the work of Christ and a desire to show the world the greatness of Jesus Christ. We don't minister to gain glory for ourselves. We minister to gain glory for our Christ.

This is why you can be hospitable with very little. It has nothing to do with whether your home can grace the cover of *Southern Living*. It's about giving people Jesus when they step through your front door. It's about meeting their needs (emotional or physical) and helping them see Christ to a greater degree.

Seasons, They Come and Go

Displaying Christ to others is why the home matters, regardless of your season in life. The Bible's commands to be hospitable and care about our homes are not isolated to middle class, married, stay-at-home moms.

McCulley and Shank divide a woman's life into twenty-year increments.[9] Each twenty years represents a season of a woman's life, give or take. Your identity does not change from season to season. Your purpose does not change. But the challenge in each particular season is discovering what God has for you.

Each season provides a different kind of focus on the home. One woman I know has children who are all grown and no longer live in her home. Instead of using her empty nest years to play and relax, she uses her home to be a blessing to her grandchildren and children by always being available to babysit and care for them when they need a hand. My mom uses her home to regularly host people from her church. She delights in making people feel loved and welcomed by her good cooking and honest conversation. And she is always ready to help her children and grandchildren who live far away, like coming to stay with us for five weeks when our twins first came home from the NICU and then coming again for two weeks a couple of months later. She uses her season of life to be available to those who are in need.

For a mom with children still at home, the home is a place of training and care. No one can replace a parent. And while having children at home in no way removes the command to be hospitable to all, it does limit the freedom of such endeavors. Before our twins were born, my husband and I loved having people over for lunch on Sundays. We considered it part of our weekend routine. But when our twins arrived, life turned upside down in many ways. After a five-week stay in the NICU followed by months of just trying to get our bearings, we began to feel like we were isolated from our church family and sorely lacking in the hospitality area. But we knew we could not maintain a Sunday lunch routine like we had before. We needed to adjust to a new season. At first, we would have people over once a month or every other month after the boys went to bed. We would have dessert and play games—two things we very much enjoy. Then as we felt more comfortable actually doing a meal, we would have people over for dinner after the boys went to bed. Now that the boys eat regular meals with us, we have entered a new phase where we can have people over while we eat as a family (although we still occasionally have dinner after they go to bed so we can actually hear the conversation). We've had to adjust. We didn't try to keep up the pace of our life prekids. But we didn't write off hospitality completely either. We want to teach our children the value of the home being a place of refuge and hospitality.

Maybe you are single and think this whole hospitality thing can't be for you. Whenever you hear people talk about the home, it's usually in the context of wives and mothers, and you naturally feel left out. Perhaps you have a full-time job that demands a lot of your time and attention, and you think that you simply can't add one more thing to your plate. Or you might live in an apartment or house with roommates and frankly, it feels awkward having people over to a single woman's house. Let me encourage you with an example from a friend of mine. You met her in chapter 1.

Andrea has lived in a house with a few other girls for some years now. In fact, she owns the house. She is well acquainted with the work that goes into owning and keeping a home. But she understands the purpose of her home. For years now, whenever a friend has needed a place for a visitor to stay, her home has been the go-to place. The women who live in this house have made countless friends over the years simply by opening up their home to traveling guests. From grilling on a summer night to hosting a small group, their home is a revolving door of friends, family, and just plain fun. The neighborhood kids are now in on it, too. While every girl in this house works a full- or part-time job, they all are ready to welcome guests at any point. Their hospitality is not just known among their friends and neighbors, but among their church family as well. People feel loved and welcomed at their house.

My goal is not to give you one more ideal to live up to. My goal is to show you that seasons vary, and each season of life requires different things. The hard part is figuring out what you can feasibly do in any given season and then implementing it. That is where wisdom comes in. The purpose of the home doesn't change. Just how you function in it does.

There is more to the home than simply being a stay-at-home mom, though that is a good thing (I am one!). Caring for the home is not a job description as much as it is a lifestyle of service. You can value and use your home for God's glory in whatever season you find yourself.

An Endless Debate

We have already seen that we were made to work. Some of us work outside the home, some of us don't. But it seems like we are always in an endless debate about the merit of both endeavors. And both sides have gotten wounded by the bullets of rhetoric. But I want to share frankly for a minute. Feminism promised that we could have an endless amount of choices and somehow still keep all the plates spinning. Feminism promised that a woman could have a home life and a work life and that by doing both she would find herself. But deep down we know we can't do this and have probably experienced the lack of fulfillment in the pursuit. Something has to give.

When you have small children at home, the home is more than a full-time job. Numerous circumstances do not allow a mom to stay home, so don't hear me saying that if you are in that situation, you are in the wrong. You have to take care of your family, and the church should do everything it can to help you in this season. But I want to speak to the mom who is trying to have it all. You don't need the income, but you like the freedom it gives you. You like the power and prestige your job gives you. You just can't find that same experience playing with toddlers and scrubbing toilets. And if someone were to really press you, you might confess that you never really liked kids before you had them. You love your own children desperately, but it's more difficult to find joy in motherhood than you anticipated. Maybe you don't have children yet, but you are on a trajectory to this very same outcome. You plan to keep your career going at full speed once your children come along.

Let me make an honest confession: you're right. Working outside of the home is a lot more prestigious than changing your fifth dirty diaper for the day (or hour!). Young children do not provide the kind of stimulating conversation that a lunch with your office colleagues affords. Cooking a meal, sweeping the floors, and opening your home to others doesn't always showcase your gifts in the ways you would like them to. But just as the home isn't supposed to be your source of identity, your career isn't either. You can serve your family with reckless abandon not because you get your fulfillment in those things ultimately, but because you have been served by Christ and you want to live for him. The problem with trying to do it all is that it makes life all about you. As we've been uncovering, God created us in his image. He wants us to tell a story about himself and not about how much we can handle, how immaculate our home is, or how hard we work in our careers.

Like McCulley and Shank say, we would do well to understand the particular season of life we are in and order our lives accordingly. Feminism sold us the lie that we could do anything we wanted to do. We could have children and a growing career. But women are tired. I think some of the exhaustion of trying to have it all is due in part to a misunderstanding of our season and the constraints and freedoms that come along with it. As you think about your role in your home, think about your particular season of life and remember one really important thing: it's only a season. There will come a day when this season will end, and then you will move on to another season. Perhaps that season will provide more freedom to do the things you have put off in this particular season. Perhaps it will have more limits. As you think through your season of life, ask God for wisdom to help you discern what is best for you in this time.

One of the popular critiques of complementarians is that we make the home ultimate. I can see how people might come to that conclusion. But that's never been what it's about. The home is not the pinnacle of greatness—Christ is. God cares about our home because so much of life happens there. God cares about our home because the home is to be a place where we work hard to showcase his glory, not our stuff. This has implications for every woman, regardless of her season. The home is about and for God.

Restoration in My Life

The home is to be a place of hospitality—for every woman. Regardless of where you are in life, the home matters. While your identity is not meant to be found there, your heart should be oriented toward the home.

For the Single Woman

Think through your season of life and what is reasonably possible, and ask God to give you wisdom to best know how to use your home for the good of others right now. Maybe it is through inviting a family over for dinner or lunch. Maybe it is through caring for a young mother's children while she runs errands or goes on a date with her husband. Maybe it is through allowing a missionary family to stay with you while they are on furlough. You can find creative ways to serve through your home in this season of your life.

For the Married Woman with No Children Living at Home

Whether your children are grown and out of the house or you haven't had them yet, you are in a season that allows you a little more freedom. It might be tempting to use this freedom solely to advance your career or enjoy long-awaited leisure and rest. Those are not bad things in and of themselves—it is good to work hard in your job, and the Bible says we need rest. But we are also called to be "others" oriented. Your home matters, kids or no kids. Perhaps you can also serve by bringing a meal to an elderly member of your church or to a neighbor who recently had surgery. You could invite another couple over for a game night at your house or host a small group from church. Think about what you enjoy and invite others into your life to enjoy it with you.

For the Mother with Children

These are precious years that you don't get back. Think carefully about your choices before you act on them. Your home is meant to be a place of productivity, so ask God where you are most productive for his glory. Work outside of the home is not always bad. Often it is necessary and helpful to a family. But consider the purpose and motive behind your work and remember the purpose of your home as well. Is there a woman in your church who you enjoy meeting with? Invite her over to share in your daily life or enjoy a cup of coffee when your kids are sleeping. Teach your children the meaning of work as you wash the dishes, fold the laundry, finish a project, or prepare dinner for your family.

Study Questions

1. Has your understanding of the home differed from the biblical definition of the home? How?

2. As God's image-bearers, how can we use our homes to demonstrate God's character to a watching world?

3. How have you struggled with a misunderstanding of what productivity in the home looks like?

4. Do you find your identity in your home or in your work? What are some evidences of this and how does Christ change your identity?

5. Review the practical application from the "Restoration in My Life" section. If you feel comfortable, share those examples or write them down.

6

Women in the Church

I've always been interested in issues surrounding gender. As an English major in college, I devoured feminist literary theory. I still remember the first time I heard of the concept of feminist theory—and something just clicked for me. I wanted more. I read every piece of literature through my feminist bent, and it all seemed to make sense to me. After I became a Christian, my fascination with gender issues transformed into understanding how women fit into the church and life. Can they preach? Can they work in a corporate setting? Can they lead men? Because of the nature of my upbringing, I did not have a hard time coming to the conclusion that the Bible has a design for us as male and female, but I know (and respect) a lot of women who do.

As I grew as a believer, my love for all things gender-related led me to study people who thought like me as well as people who thought differently. I attended lectures, gatherings, and debates in my city that brought to light the very questions I was pondering and did so from a biblical point of view. It was here that I came face to face with the struggle many earnest women have with a particular topic in God's Word: the role of women in the church. What can they do? What can't they do?

I was confronted head-on with these very questions years ago during an egalitarian roundtable discussion at a local Christian university in Minneapolis. As the lone complementarian, I felt out of place, but very welcomed. I wanted to hear the other side of this issue. I didn't want to be at the mercy of other people's definitions of egalitarianism and feminism. I wanted to understand those definitions from a firsthand encounter. As the young women talked about their strong desires for ministry in the local church, a common theme kept emerging.

They didn't so much like the apostle Paul.

These women loved God's Word and wanted to believe it was true, but they struggled over the frequency and strength of Paul's qualifications for pastors/elders in the church. When they read 1 Timothy 2:12, "I do not permit a woman to teach or to exercise authority over a man; rather, she is to remain quiet," they felt slighted. When they saw that Paul restricted the office of elder/pastor to qualified men, their spirits were crushed. They felt this strong urge to serve God in a leadership capacity, but couldn't see where they could fit in a local church.

I've also known women who don't feel called to teach the Bible. They possess useful gifts of service, administration, and mercy. With all of the pressure and emphasis on teaching, however, sometimes they feel out of place. Do their gifts matter, too?

Feminism promised to give women options that were better than what they had been previously offered. This has led to women believing they should be able to do anything they want in the local church. And when confronted with the biblical pattern for church leadership or service in the church, feminism pushes women to do more and assert their rights. But the biblical pattern for the local church is not about any person's rights.

The Purpose of the Church

Before we go any further in our discussion of the local church, we need to get clear on something vitally important.

God has a purpose for the local church. And we don't get to change that purpose.

True, there are many good, smaller purposes for a local congregation, and they look different in each context. But God has set forth one overarching purpose of the church.

Mark Dever defines the purpose of the local church in this way:

> The end and purpose of all of this [leadership in the church] is the glory of God as we make Him known. Throughout history, God has desired to make Himself known. This is why He delivered Israel from Egypt in the Exodus, and why He delivered them again from the Babylonian Exile. It was for His own glory, to make Himself known . . . He has created the world and has done all that He has done for His own praise. And it is right and good that He should do so. . . . All who read these words—those who are church leaders and those who are not—are made in the image of God. We are to be walking pictures of the moral nature and righteous character of God, reflecting it around the universe for all to see—especially in our union with God through Christ. This, therefore is what God calls us to and why He calls us to it. He calls us to join together with Him, and together in our congregations, not for our glory but for His own.[1]

As we saw in chapter 1, God cares about what story we tell with our lives. We are his image-bearers. Our very lives, for better or worse, tell a story of him—and this carries over into how we act in the local church. The local church images God collectively as we image him individually. And the world is watching.

As Dever said, every facet of this universe is God's to claim and to direct. Psalm 24:1–2 says, "The earth is the Lord's and the fullness thereof, the world and those who dwell therein, for he has founded it upon the seas and established it upon the rivers." He created all things, sustains all things, and owns all things. This even has implications for how we function within his church.

God created us, and we belong to him. We do not dictate how we are to live, God does. Paul says in 1 Timothy 2:13–14 that Adam and Eve were created. By whom? The Lord God himself.

Again, in 1 Corinthians 11:11, we see that even though a woman is made from man and a man is born of a woman—they both come from God. The entire Bible is God's overarching directive for us—beginning with the first command in Genesis to the last in Revelation. God has created us for his glory—and there is a way in which we are to live.

Not only did God create us for his glory, but he is also sovereign over every inch of his creation (Psalm 104). Everything that God has created is rightfully his and he rules it—including us. With his sovereignty comes his authority over his creation (Col. 1:16). It is this power to create and rule perfectly that gives him authority over us (James 1:18). Our understanding of all other authority comes from our understanding of God's authority. If we do not believe that he has the authority to prescribe boundaries for us, then we will have a hard time making sense of the commands that we are about to study regarding our involvement in the local church.

But he is not sitting back and directing us like pawns. He is lovingly guiding us to delight in living for his glory. All of his commands are not burdensome for the one who is in Christ. They are life and joy (Ps. 119:40, 93). Our reaction to his authority in our lives should be one of gratitude and willing service for the glory of his name (Luke 1:38).

As Dever said, one of the means God uses to manifest his glory is through the local church. We should see it as an immense privilege to be among God's people in service, worship, and fellowship. Paul explains to Timothy why he gives his commands: "So that . . . you may know how one ought to behave in the household of God, which is the church of the living God, a pillar and buttress of truth" (1 Tim. 3:15). This is you and me. We are a part of the church of the living God. We are to be a pillar and buttress of truth when we gather with God's people. When we gather together to worship with other believers, we are a living, breathing testimony of the absolute goodness, authority, and sovereignty of our creator, God.

To further understand the purpose of the local church, let me bring in some more reinforcements. Ligon Duncan and Susan Hunt give three qualities of the local church as seen in 1 Timothy 3:15:[2]

1. The local church is the household of God—the family of God.
2. The local church is the church of the living God—he assembles among us.
3. The local church is the pillar and buttress of truth—we are to be the vehicle for evangelism and discipleship, and the defender of the faith.

Both 1 Timothy and 1 Corinthians were written to churches. Paul knew how important the church was for the gospel and for Christians. The health and life of the local church was, and still is, vital for gospel ministry—and this includes how men and women relate to one another. Paul regularly brings up gender in his letters to local churches because how we understand our manhood and womanhood matters in even the seemingly insignificant details that pertain to a local church. How we relate to one another in the local church speaks volumes about the gospel and about God's Word. Paul is speaking as an authoritative voice on behalf of God, showing that our design as male and female is crucial not only in the home, but also in the church.

Wayne Grudem states it this way:

> Leadership patterns in the family will reflect leadership patterns in the church, and vice versa. . . . As godly men fulfill their leadership responsibilities in the family, they should also fulfill leadership responsibilities in the church. Conversely, if patterns of female leadership are established in the church, it will inevitably bring pressure toward greater female leadership, and toward abdication of male leadership, within the family.[3]

Just as God's glory can be seen in his design for the family and marriage, his glory is revealed in how men and women respond to each other in the local church. Men and women in marriage reflect God's covenant love between Christ and his bride, the church.

Within the walls of your local congregation, this metaphor is further realized in how leadership is ordered and functions. God is telling a story about himself through two earthly realities, marriage and the local church. And he is the one who decides how the story goes.

My Purpose in the Local Church

We will get to the obvious elephant in the room in the next section, but before we talk about women's specific roles in the local church, I think it would be helpful to first talk about the overarching purpose for all women in the local church: we are to use the gifts God has given us. I often hear that the Bible's teaching on women in the church banishes women to the nurseries and kitchens and prevents them from *truly* using their gifts. Friends, this is a dangerous attitude. Just as feminism has told women that anything a man can do women can do just the same, it has encouraged women to clamor *only* for what men do, and to belittle "traditional" women's activities. In the church, women often conclude that the gifts of service are not as important as the gifts of teaching. In the same way that the message of feminism sometimes maligns motherhood and marriage, the message of feminism in the church sometimes maligns the gifts of service that so many of God's people joyfully possess. If someone says that women are "just" relegated to rocking babies and making casseroles for a potluck, then what does that communicate to the woman who truly is gifted in those very needed ministries in the church? Does she feel as valued as the woman who teaches? She should, my friends. She absolutely should.

The Bible has a better way for us to think about women in the church. According to God's Word, there is room in the church for all of us to use our gifts—and they all have value. The Corinthian church had the same faulty attitude toward gifts in the church. In 1 Corinthians 12:1–14:40, Paul corrects their thinking that one gift is better than another. By using the human body as his example, he shows that, like every part of our physical bodies, all spiritual gifts are necessary for the local church to truly flourish. We need our heart and brain just as much as our mouth and hands. Without both the visible and less visible members of our physical bodies, we function at a lesser capacity. The same is true for the local church. We need the teaching gifts *and* the gifts of service and administration.

So what does this mean for you? It means you serve a vital purpose in your local church.

The church where my husband and I serve is a young church plant. At the time when I'm writing this book, we have only been in existence for three years. So you can imagine that there are a lot of needs to be met. Many spiritual gifts line up with the everyday needs in our church. We have members who serve in the nursery. We have members who bring food for our hospitality table. We have members who greet people as they arrive on Sunday morning. One of our pastor's wives prints the bulletins and works on a myriad of administrative needs. Members meet together for discipleship (Matt. 28:19). Older women help younger women grow in godliness (Titus 2:3–5). Others open their homes for Bible study and informal gatherings (Heb. 10:25). One of our members cleans the church every week. Sure, our pastors preach and are men, but do you see how that is only one piece of the puzzle of our local church? Without members meeting together, the Bible would not be applied as deeply. Without faithful volunteers in the nursery, moms and dads might miss the service regularly and be unable to take in the preached Word. Without someone coordinating the details of our church events (like picnics and nursery schedules), we would experience chaos and important things would be missed. Our hospitality table brings people together at the end of the service. Without the people who bring food every week, a vital component of fellowship would be missed on Sunday mornings.

The local church exists to make God known to a watching world. And we get to be part of that unfolding plan. Our purpose in the local church is not to strive for the greatest amount of power or authority, but to excel in service to God and to "outdo one another in showing honor" (Rom. 12:10). In God's economy every last one of us is useful and important. Every last one of us has been given gifts and abilities. God gave you gifts and abilities to be utilized in your local congregation. Do you always find yourself organizing things? Perhaps your gift of administration could be used to serve in your church's office. Are you always looking for ways to alleviate the needs of others? Your gift of mercy can be used to make God known to "the least of these" (Matt. 25:40). Maybe you really enjoy serving people. From helping a new mom by bringing her a meal to cleaning the apartment of an elderly member, gifts of service make the love of God tangible to those in need.

But maybe you feel gifted to teach and are wondering what that looks like for you. While I don't believe the teaching gifts are ultimate, and I think the debate surrounding them often makes them *seem* ultimate, we can't talk about feminism and the local church without talking about the elephant in the room.

What about My Gifts?

Maybe you've been reading this and have felt a lump rising in your throat. You have sensed a burning desire to teach and lead in your church for quite some time and aren't exactly sure what to do about it. Many people have told you that God has clearly gifted you to teach his Word, but then you read something like this and feel like you were made for nothing. You feel like your gifts are wasted. I can relate. I, too, feel like God has gifted me to teach, but let me encourage you with this simple truth—your gifts are not wasted.

I'm not the only one who has wrestled with this tension. Blogger Fabs Hartford has a helpful dialogue about the tension we face as women seeking to be useful and the pull of feminism all around us. In one blog post, she recounts learning that to be a conservative, complementarian woman means using one's gifts fully. I think we need more women like her. Fabs writes:

> Here's the deal: Father, Son and Spirit have different roles and they are still equal. Their worth is not defined by their tasks.

> It's our worldview—not God's—that assigns value based on role. As long as we find our worth in our to-do list, we will confuse equality and sameness.
>
> Your gifts are not wasted, dear sister. You were created female, yes. You were created to be useful. You were created to flourish. You were created to serve God with complete devotion. You were created to stand for truth, herald righteousness, and love God with every fiber of your being. But that doesn't mean those gifts don't come with parameters.[4]

But even though our gifts come with parameters, there is much freedom to serve in the local church if you feel gifted to teach. Paul tells Titus to encourage the older women to "teach what is good" (Titus 2:3). You can teach what is good through leading a small group Bible study, teaching at a women's retreat or conference, mentoring a younger woman, training other women in Bible study, leading a prayer ministry, writing Bible study curriculum, teaching children's Sunday school—and the list could go on. The point is that women who are gifted to teach have a place in the church. The church is made up of women who are hungry to know God and his Word. Those who are gifted to teach are called to help them in this pursuit.[5]

Why, then, do we feel this pull of feminism even as we serve in our local church?

First-Wave Feminism and the Church

Some have said that the first feminists were committed Christians who merely wanted voting rights and marriage equality for women. In this spirit, those same people say that feminism and Christianity can be reconciled. It is the second and third waves that hijacked feminism and made it about more than mere equality for the sexes. While we have only recently seen the push for women's leadership in the church, the roots of this idea started with the suffragists. Margaret Köstenberger has this to say about first-wave feminists and their view of Scripture:

> First-wave nineteenth century feminists used two primary methods for interpreting Scripture. The first method sought to counter the argument of those who limited the role of women by reasoning from passages that "spoke" of the equality of men and women in Christ. The second method made use of female characters in Scripture that could serve as role models for women in leadership, such as Deborah, Ruth, and Esther. Toward the end of the nineteenth century, a more critical approach began to take hold. This approach labeled the actual biblical texts as sexist and challenged their integrity, including their view of women.[6]

She goes on to say:

> The rising tide of women active in Christian ministry and scholarship reached a culmination point in The Women's Bible, edited by Elizabeth Cady Stanton (1895, 1898). The work resembles a commentary more than a translation, with twenty women contributors enlisted to comment on selected biblical passages judged significant for women.
>
> Stanton herself did not consider the Mosaic law to be inspired, yet she acknowledged the powerful influence of the Bible as the bedrock of male-dominated Western law and civilization. Believing that women's emancipation would be impossible if Scripture's position continued to be accepted, Stanton applied a supposed "higher criticism" to erode its authority, particularly with regard to biblical teaching on women.[7]

While many within the first-wave feminist movement were Christians, leaders like Stanton and others did not want to reconcile the Bible's teaching on women and women in the church with their own views on the emancipation of women. For them it was impossible for the two to go together. Today, feminists either deny the authority of Scripture or try to change its meaning in order to substantiate their views on the church. A healthy understanding of history shows us that today's seemingly novel ideas are really nothing new.

In the spirit of first-wave feminists, like Stanton, many mainline Protestant denominations now ordain women. Women are now sitting in seminary classrooms across the country training for pastoral ministry. It is not uncommon to see a woman standing in a pulpit preaching to men. While in some parts of the country, and segments of evangelicalism, this is still a foreign concept, I imagine that in the next ten to fifteen years we will see an even greater rise of women filling elder/pastor roles in local congregations.

For Men Only

Once we understand the purpose of the local church, we are better equipped to understand why this whole gender thing matters. What does the Bible say about women in the local church? Remember how I talked about Paul in the beginning of the chapter? I agree with my egalitarian friends: he has a lot of black-and-white stuff to say about women in the church. Let's look at a few passages.

One of the most startling statements that Paul makes is found in 1 Timothy 2:11–12:

> Let a woman learn quietly with all submissiveness. I do not permit a woman to teach or to exercise authority over a man; rather she is to remain quiet.

This can sound really harsh and misogynistic in our age of personal autonomy. But as Christians, we are all under authority. The local church is under the authority of Christ. We all submit to his authority.

From the birth of the church after Christ's resurrection until now, God's intention for the local church has been for godly, qualified men to lead his people through the preaching and teaching of his Word.

When we hear this, some of us have flashbacks to a time when men sat in dark rooms, smoked cigars, and kept up the "good old boy network." This is not how God intends for his church to function. Consider Paul's qualifications for elders.

> The saying is trustworthy: If anyone aspires to the office of overseer, he desires a noble task. Therefore an overseer must be above reproach, the husband of one wife, sober-minded, self-controlled, respectable, hospitable, able to teach, not a drunkard, not violent but gentle, not quarrelsome, not a lover of money. He must manage his own household well, with all dignity keeping his children submissive, for if someone does not know how to manage his own household, how will he care for God's church? He must not be a recent convert, or he may become puffed up with conceit and fall into the condemnation of the devil. Moreover, he must be well thought of by outsiders, so that he may not fall into disgrace, into a snare of the devil. (1 Tim. 3:1–7)

> For an overseer, as God's steward, must be above reproach. He must not be arrogant or quick-tempered or a drunkard or violent or greedy for gain, but hospitable, a lover of good, self-controlled, upright, holy, and disciplined. He must hold firm to the trustworthy word as taught, so that he may be able to give instruction in sound doctrine and also to rebuke those who contradict it. (Titus 1:7–9)

These are serious matters. When God calls a man to be a pastor/elder, that calling is not to be taken lightly. It's not "come one, come all" for the men and a locked gate for the women. The local church is not a boys' club. In fact, the restriction for men to the office of elder/pastor is actually quite freeing. Why? Because the restriction applies to only *one* office. It does not apply to the entirety of ministry in a local church. As I already mentioned, there are a host of options available to women in the local church. When we hear Paul's command for women to be silent, it does not apply to all aspects of the church, but only one office. As we've already seen, the local church flourishes only to the extent that every member is working together. We should also note that the office of pastor/elder is not restricted to men; it is restricted to "qualified men." That means that many men will not qualify for this kind of service too.

Let's look at who these qualified men are. There is a general character that should mark these men. They are able to teach. They are kind. They are hospitable. They are family men who love their wives (if they have one) and their children (if they have them), and they value their homes. They are self-controlled. They are holy. They love God's Word and his people. In every sense of the word, they are *different*. Different from the world and even different from your average guy off the street. They are marked by God's undeniable call on their life.

I first wrestled through what gender roles look like in the church when I was in college. I remember the first time I didn't know how to answer someone who challenged my new belief that God reserved the role of pastor/elder for qualified men. She pressed me and pressed me, and I came up short. In my head I knew I was right, but the words just wouldn't come. I was speechless (and that's rare for a talker like me). I promised myself that I would never again be left speechless about what I believed God's Word teaches. So my dad helped me out. He compared the qualifications for elders/pastors to the Old Testament qualifications for priest. Do you remember what those were? Among many other things addressed in the Pentateuch, Moses restricts the role of priest to one tribe—the Levites. So what if a godly, gifted Benjamite boy dreams of becoming a priest? He can't. God didn't make him a Levite. God had a plan and a purpose for how he wanted his people to function so he would get the most glory and they would get the most joy. Being created as male or female or Benjamite or Levite is not an occasion for discontent or frustration with God's design. It's a chance to be humbled, and to then flourish in how he created you. We get joy when we obey God and function within his intended framework. The same is true for how the local church is meant to be structured.[8]

A Place at the Table

We are all familiar with the regulations that require equal work for equal pay. In our society today, employers are required by law to pay a woman the same wage as if the job were filled by a man. Women cannot be discriminated against based on their gender. In fact, gender cannot be a factor in determining whether a person should be hired at all. These are all helpful and good products of feminism. There was a time not too long ago when being a woman had immediate, inherent, and unfair disadvantages; as I've said before, some of the results of feminism are good and necessary. But many feminists argue that we should view the local church as an equal opportunity employer.

God doesn't work that way. In God's economy, equality does not mean sameness.

Whenever feminists talk about opportunities for women, they liken it to a need to have a seat at the proverbial table—the table of cultural power, leadership, and masculinity.

In order for women to fully arrive, they need to be offered equal footing. In feminist thinking, this means giving a gifted woman the pulpit. Anything less is at best unfair and at worst oppression.

This is classic "equality equals sameness" thinking that has defined the feminist movement for over a century. I clung to this kind of thinking too, at one point. Whenever I heard a man say I couldn't do something because I was female or too emotional or whatever, my back stiffened and my determination rose. *Of course I can do that. I am a woman and I am equal. Anything you can do, I can do better.*

Mary Kassian has this to say about feminism in the church:

> The mainstreaming of feminist thought has profound implications for the church. Over the past ten years, the ordination of women (and homosexuals) to the office of elder/bishop/pastor, inclusive language, womanist liturgy, feminist theology, and feminist hermeneutics have become commonplace. Even the evangelical church has witnessed popularization of the ordination of women, inclusive language, and most recently challenges and changes to historic Trinitarian doctrine. But by far, the most noticeable shift in the church in the past ten years is in the

> "default" understanding of male and female roles. In generations past, individuals generally understood and accepted that God assigned the male a unique spiritual role in the governance and guidance of the home and church. Distinctive, complementary roles for male and female were supported in both thought and practice. By default, complementarity was regarded as the right, good, and natural order of creation.
>
> The feminist tsunami changed all that. Feminism maintains that equality necessitates role interchangeability—a woman cannot be a man's equal unless she can assume the same role as he. This philosophy of egalitarianism is well on its way to thorough acceptance in the evangelical church.
>
> Egalitarianism maintains that there is no unique position of spiritual authority reserved for men in the church or home. Women can and ought to assume all positions freely. Egalitarianism is the "default setting" of the new millennium.[9]

Kassian wrote the updated version of this book in 2005, but as you can see, our current culture is no different. Feminism, as we have seen in every other part of our life, is in our blood now. Feminism used to be something you had to ascribe to intentionally. Now it's so much a part of us that we have to intentionally turn from it in order to understand God's good design for us.

The purpose of the local church is not to benefit ourselves. What we do in the church has nothing to do with our rights and everything to do with God's glory. Feminism, at its core, is about rights and authority. The local church, at its core, is about God and his authority over us. He has gifted each of us in unique ways. Our gifts find their home in humble service in a local congregation, not when we are clamoring for authority or pitting one gift against another.

Restoration in My Life

There is a place for all of us in our local church. And not just a place, but a necessary purpose. You matter in God's economy, whether you teach in front of others or serve quietly behind the scenes.

For the Married Woman in a Busy Season of Life

Some of you are in a place in your life where the very thought of adding something else to your plate overwhelms you, but you want so badly to serve your local church. There are many possibilities for you to pour your life into ministry. *Ordinary* and *mundane* are not synonymous with *useless*. One of the ways I attempt to serve my local church is through inviting women into my daily life. I learned this from women who did this for me. Before I got married and had children, older women helped and encouraged me by simply sharing life with me. Sometimes I would spend an afternoon at the park with them and their children. Sometimes I would tag along while they ran errands. Sometimes I would have dinner with them. Throughout their busy season of life, they taught me what it looks like to love God, love your children, and love your family. In God's providence, I am now in that busy season. It's hard to think outside of the daily grind of caring for little ones and a husband. But even a simple gesture of inviting another woman over to enter your world of organized chaos is obeying God's command to teach the next generation and love your local church.

Some of you are mommies. No woman has more influence on the next generation of wives and mothers than a mother herself. For better or worse, your daughter will learn how to be a woman from you—and you can either be intentional about passing on Scripture's teaching of what true womanhood is, or you can allow her to learn by default from the world. This is your highest ministry to the local church. You are raising future church members and souls who will never die. You are given a firsthand opportunity to obey the teachings of Titus 2:3–5 every single day.

Maybe you are gifted to teach, but aren't sure how that fits into your schedule. Start small. Perhaps starting a blog to write your thoughts discipling just one woman can give you the outlet needed to exercise these gifts. And remember, it's just a season.

For the Single or Married Woman Working Outside the Home

I know that it can feel overwhelming to support yourself and serve in your local church. If you are single and have children, it can be even more challenging. But whether you believe it right now or not, your singleness is a gift from the Lord, and he does not want you to waste it. Your childlessness is a gift from the Lord, and he does not want you to waste it. The world would have you spend your "free time" on your pursuits and your desires, but God owns you—and God owns your singleness and childlessness. Singleness affords a freedom to serve in a way unlike any other status. Your womanhood is not based on your marital status. It's not based on how many children you have. Rather, you are a woman by birth. Therefore, these principles apply very much to you. Your calling to disciple women and children can manifest itself in many ways. It might mean babysitting for a young mother while she takes a morning or evening off. It might mean babysitting for that same family while mom and dad have a date night. The Lord has brought many "older women" into my life simply through watching their kids. I have been greatly blessed by watching them live and soaking up their wisdom. And, remember that you are an older woman to someone, so use God's gift of singleness to pour your life into that of another. Maybe there is a younger woman in your church that you connect with. If you feel gifted to teach, ask your pastor or women's ministry leader if there are opportunities for you to test and exercise this gift. You will be blessed in a multitude of ways by your willingness to serve. John Piper says that the unwasted life is one that "puts the infinite value of Christ on display for the world to see."[10]

For the Married Woman in a Quieter Season of Life

Maybe you have older children or are in a season of life that is less crazy. Many newly married women or young moms are so wrapped up in their new roles that they cannot think in terms of being mentored. I encourage you to make it simple—just invite them over to talk. Maybe you can offer to teach a new wife how to cook or grocery shop on a budget. God has brought you to this place in your life so you can share it with others. There is a woman in our church whose daughters are grown and married. She doesn't waste the free time she has in this season of her life. She serves her elderly mother. She ministers to the sick and hurting. She is eager to evangelize those who do not know Christ and invests in friendships with them. She sacrifices her time to help me with my twin boys. She studies God's Word and has a passion to see other women do the same. She freely ministers and serves God's people because she believes in the purpose of the local church and the power of God's Word.

Do you believe that the local church is God's means of getting his glory to the ends of the earth and desire to be a part of the effort? There is a place for you, sister! Perhaps your church needs a new Bible study teacher, or maybe they need a Bible study for women altogether. Or maybe your church needs someone to lead a mercy ministry to refugees, women considering abortion, or trafficking victims, and you have always felt a passion for the least of these. Maybe you are particularly gifted in finance and administration, and your church is looking for someone to keep their books or provide counsel for the church budget. We are all gifted in a variety of capacities. In our function as image-bearers, we bring important and distinct qualities to the local church table.

Study Questions

1. Do you struggle with the apostle Paul, like the women in the story at the beginning of the chapter? If so, how does understanding God's purpose for the local church shed new light on your struggle?

2. How do you think your gifts can be used in your local church? Do you think feminism has influenced your appreciation of those gifts?

3. How are restrictions for women in the church actually freeing? How does that help you serve your local church?

4. How does "equality does not mean sameness" work itself out in the life of the church? How do the different roles men and women play in the local church give God glory?

7

Restoration Is Possible

Life is demanding. So many things vie for your attention on any given day. A project at work. An article to finish and send to your editor. A baby who needs to be nursed and a toddler who needs to be read to. A husband who needs your love and attention. A friend who needs a listening ear. A church that is looking for more women to serve. A neighbor who is struggling with the news that her husband just left her and comes to you for help. As women, it can feel like we are constantly pulled in a variety of directions that all seem to have the same level of urgency. We're left not knowing exactly where to start or what to focus on. When one plate starts spinning, another falls.

And if we are truly honest, we feel like we don't really measure up to this whole godly woman thing. It all feels too hard sometimes. Too demanding.

I remember a conversation with a dear friend that helped bring this tension to light for me. This friend has a servant's heart that radiates love for people. She is always quick to offer to come to my house to play with my twin boys and help me where needed. When my husband travels, she will come in the afternoon to keep me company or allow me to run errands that are difficult to accomplish with two busy one-year-olds. After I had minor surgery and was unable to lift my boys for a few days, she came over in the mornings to help me with even the most basic tasks, like lifting them on to the changing table or putting them in their high chairs for lunch. (You never know how much you need your lifting capabilities until you are medically required not to use them!) If I could pick one word to describe this friend, it would be *cheerful*. When she comes to help me, she does it with eagerness and joy. I imagine it is not easy to give up your day off from work for someone else. I could think of a million things I would rather do if I had a day off. But she comes to serve. She comes to help. She enters into my life and encourages me.

Why do I mention her? Because in the midst of all her joyful service, I have regularly heard her recount how much she needs to learn to apply aspects of womanhood better. While I see Christ so evidently displayed in her sacrifice for me, she only sees a failure to measure up to the "ideal woman" who keeps a perfectly clean home and cooks a hearty meal every night. She feels the weight of this call to being a godly woman and wants to live rightly.

If my friend—who has so blessed and encouraged me by her example—is struggling with this, I think it's safe to say that the competing voices we hear as women are affecting all of us. We hear from the culture that we must break the glass ceiling and go where no woman has gone before. We hear from our friends and acquaintances that the measure of a woman is in her ability to have children or her disposition toward her husband—but many don't have children or a husband. We hear on the news that women deserve equal pay and the right to make choices for themselves. We hear in the church that if women are equal, then they should be free to exercise their gifts in any capacity they choose.

Do you ever feel overwhelmed by it all? Do you ever look at yourself in the mirror and think to yourself, *this womanhood thing is not for the faint of heart*. I feel you. Even though in the depth of my soul I believe the Bible teaches that God has a good design for us as women, I struggle with the application of it sometimes. When Christ saved me, I saw so many old parts of my life fade away. I was a new creation. But like Paul in Romans 7, the good I want to do, I don't always do. The old woman is still wrestling with the new woman. And to be honest, I sometimes feel like a complete failure on the womanhood front.

In the midst of writing this book, I suffered a miscarriage. It was my second one, so you would think that I would have anticipated the feelings of despair and grief that came in the moments, weeks, and months after we heard the awful words, "There is no heartbeat." But I didn't. For a number of reasons, it was a more complicated miscarriage than my first, and the grief was much more prolonged than we anticipated. It lingered. The sadness covered me like a heavy, wet blanket. In moments of difficulty, we are usually given a glimpse of our true selves, aren't we? For me, that is when the real Courtney comes out. In those weeks following our miscarriage, the real Courtney was not a pretty sight to behold. In a night of complete despair, I looked at my husband and told him, "I am not qualified to write this book." The Bible says that a woman who hopes in God is truly beautiful. She is a godly woman. On that night, I wasn't there. Not by a long shot. As the grief settled in around me and my emotions overtook me, every part of me felt like a fraud when it came to writing about godly womanhood. I knew I wasn't measuring up to the standard set forth in Scripture. (I do not think it is ever helpful to assess our ability to measure up to standards in the midst of overwhelming grief. We will most likely always fall short in those times.) What my husband so helpfully reminded me in those moments is that my feelings could not be trusted, and I should not assess my spiritual growth as I mourned our loss. Those are helpful words for anyone in such a devastating trial. But it didn't remove the fact that I felt like a fraud.

I have experienced this weakness in less tragic circumstances as well. As you might have picked up, marriage rocked me to the core. I struggled with submission. I struggled with respecting and trusting my husband. I struggled with incorporating my life into his. Prior to marriage, however, I was a champion for all things godly womanhood. Three days after saying "I do," however, I was ready to crawl into a corner and give up on thinking that I knew so much.

I am not the model. But the model was never meant to be you or me anyway. I've got a newsflash for you: perfection is not attainable. Perfection was only attained by one person, Christ. We have something better than the girl next door or an evangelical Martha Stewart. We have Jesus. We have the holy and inspired Word of God that contains all we need for life and godliness.

We can't even get close. We will never be the Proverbs 31 woman, because she wasn't a real person. She is a model of a virtuous woman, not the picture-perfect woman we have in our heads. We will never reach that level of perfection in our lifetime. Throughout this book, I've tried to provide hope for change, but please know that we will never do it all perfectly. My temptation when I am confronted with my failings (and they are many) is to retreat. I want to just give up. I determine that my sin is the final word. Maybe you can relate.

But I've got a better newsflash for you: your sin is not the final word. Mine isn't either.

While the culture (and even the church sometimes) spends its energy trying to help women figure out how to have it all, we need to remember the healing balm of the gospel when we work with all our might and find that we come up short. Think about your standing before God. In Christ, all of your sins are forgiven (Eph. 1:17; Col. 1:13–14). In Christ, you have been given a new nature—his nature that is free from sin (2 Cor. 5:17). In Christ, his righteousness is credited to your account, so when God looks at you, he doesn't see your sin and failure to measure up to his commands; he sees his perfect and holy Son (Heb. 10:17). Do you see how wonderful this news is for you, dear sister? When you place your head on the pillow at the end of another wearying day, you can rest in the fact that while your sins might scream condemnation at you, Jesus is saying, "It is finished!" (John 19:30). There is no more condemnation left for you. All that is required of you is repentance and faith (Acts

3:19; 1 John 1:9). This is abundantly freeing as we seek to apply the truths of God's design to our own lives. Maybe sometimes we take one step forward and two steps back. But we can rest in the sure promise that the same Christ who accomplished this good work of salvation in us will finish the work he started (Phil. 1:6). The gospel assures us that we will make it to that final day when we see our Savior face to face (1 Thess. 5:23–24). It is powerful over our sin, our failure to measure up, and even our prideful assumption that we have it all together.

Maybe you do not feel like a failure as a woman. You look at your life and your chest swells with confidence. You have made something of yourself. You are doing it all. The gospel is for you, too, sister. The truth is, whether you think you are strong or know you are weak, the verdict still comes back the same on us all—guilty. The best things we accomplish are all owing to grace. Proverbs 16:18 says that "pride goes before destruction and a haughty spirit before a fall." Your boasting in your own ability is really the prelude to your humbling. Your best days are all owing to God's grace. There is nothing that you and I do that is not enabled by the amazing grace of God (John 15:5).

Feminism and the Gospel

But since this is a book on how feminism impacts womanhood, you might be wondering how the gospel has anything to do with feminism. You get how the gospel gives us hope in our weakness, but feminism is an ideology. How does the gospel have anything to say about that? As an ideology, feminism is rooted in an understanding of the world. Feminism views the world through the female lens, sometimes to the exclusion of men. If we believe that men and women are equally created in the image of God, then we must believe that to view the world through one particular gender's lens and draw life-altering conclusions from that worldview (to the exclusion of the other gender) is contrary to God's design for his creation.

The Bible show us that men and women are different because together they showcase God's image. Feminism claims otherwise. Feminism claims to be the answer for the oppression of women, but nothing frees women like the gospel of Jesus Christ. Some feminists even claim that Jesus was a card-carrying feminist himself, but the seeds of feminism are actually an affront to the gospel. While some results of feminism have been good for society, the overarching message of cultural feminism is damaging. Feminism falsely asserts that equality equals sameness and that I am my own authority. While some might claim that feminism is historically Christian, a more robust understanding of the history of the women's movement reveals that while the push for women to be able to vote, own property, and have equal legal standing with men accomplished necessary things for women, other teaching about womanhood that was born out of this movement is contrary to God's Word. As we saw in the previous chapter, some of the feminists who fought so hard for a woman's right to vote also wanted to discard biblical teaching on women in an effort to get them into pulpits and out from under the authority of their husbands.

At the end of the day, we can trust that God's Word has spoken clearly on the matter of womanhood. And we are not God's interpreter. He is.

So how does the gospel shatter all of these false understandings of womanhood? I believe it's in the same way that it frees us from our feelings of inadequacy. It makes us new creations.

Satan wants nothing more than to keep us in a state of thinking that our personal autonomy and right to our own authority is paramount. He hates the image that we portray. He hates God, and he will stop at nothing to make us question God's goodness and design. What happens if we get womanhood wrong? If our womanhood is meant to tell a story about God and his glory in creation, about God and his good design, about God and his purpose in making us image-bearers, then womanhood matters significantly. It has eternal and spiritual implications that go beyond our mere ability to preach on a Sunday morning or whether we submit to our husbands. When we get womanhood wrong, we tell a wrong story about Christ's relationship with his bride. We tell a wrong story about God. We essentially say that God has not really spoken. That is Satan's biggest tactic, isn't it? To get us to say, "Has God really said?" Eve believed the lie and we are prone to believe it too.

But in Christ, we have hope. We have the promise that God has absolutely spoken, and he has spoken with authority through his Son, Jesus. Restoring our delight in God's design means nothing if we aren't trusting in Christ alone for the forgiveness of our sins and our only hope for righteousness. If you read this book and resolve to do better tomorrow, but never get on your knees and beg God for the grace to do so, then all of your efforts are filthy rags before him. You might be living some form of womanhood, but it won't be biblical. A biblical woman is rooted in the finished work of Christ. A biblical woman knows that the only way she is going to live for God and live as his image-bearer is through the merit of his Son. Christ lived perfectly so we don't have to. Because let's face it, we know we never will.

Womanhood Is Theology in Practice

It is not popular these days to say that men and women were made for different roles and functions. Even in evangelical circles, I have heard some women approach the topic of womanhood with hesitancy. It's not that they don't believe it is true. It's not even that they don't value God's Word. They do, very much. But because of the wars that have been fought over this issue, they would rather focus their attention elsewhere. They don't want to get in a battle. And quite frankly, they have encountered far too many women who can recite Proverbs 31 and the other passages about women, but who don't know the slightest thing about what they mean. They want women to devour the meat of God's Word with an insatiable hunger. They want women to love theology and crave the study of God and his ways. I want that, too. I went to seminary for that very reason. I was raised by a mom who is a theologian in her own right. The very fact that I am writing a book and read like I do is because I learned from her that theology matters. So the effort to encourage women to study deep things is not lost on me. I am in this battle with you, but not to the exclusion of biblical womanhood. I think that both need to go together. Why? Understanding God's design is theology in practice. When we apply the biblical teaching of God's design for us as women to our daily lives, whatever season of life we are in, we are doing practical theology. We are taking God at his Word. James says that faith without works is dead (James 2:14–26). So is theology. As we study theology, we should grow in a number of practical ways. Growing in godly womanhood matters because the Bible matters. This is why studying only about womanhood is not enough. We need all of Scripture in order to grow. But the truth of God's good design for us matters, and shouldn't be limited in our study or abandoned completely.

That is what this entire book has been about—theology in practice. God's Word is true, so we act on it. The gospel is sufficient, so we have grace to fight our sin and move forward. Our womanhood matters because it tells a story about God and his Word. Don't buy into the argument that you need to avoid talking about being a woman. You don't. The world around us hasn't given up on setting forth a model for womanhood. Neither should we. Feminism is alive and well inside and outside of the church. If we believe that a right understanding of womanhood images God, then we can't afford to be silent on this issue.

Your Womanhood Is Not on Hold

What if you feel stuck? What if you are waiting to get married or waiting to have children? What if you are between jobs? What if you haven't found a church yet? What if you are in college or recently graduated and living with your parents? You feel like you're in limbo. You want to put this theology into practice, but it feels useless. You aren't where you thought you would be at this point in your life.

My life hasn't always gone the way I planned it to go. I thought I would be married by the time I graduated from college. I wasn't. I thought for sure I would have at least two children by my ten-year high school reunion. I didn't have any. While I got married a few years after college, the quest to have children was far more difficult than I had imagined. Instead, as I moved into my late twenties, I found myself teaching a marriage and family class to high school students, rather than teaching a toddler how to say *mommy* and *daddy*.

I often felt like I was in limbo. I felt like I was less of a woman. What I wanted so desperately was to bear and nurture life, yet all I saw every month was another negative pregnancy test. Was this what defined me and my worth? Was I failing?

Throughout this book, we have looked at the many aspects of God's design for us. So I ask again, what makes a woman a woman? Is it her prowess in the kitchen or her devotion to her husband? Is it her ability to manage a variety of projects without having a meltdown, or the fact that she has given birth to a multitude of children? Or is it something more than that? How do you grow as a woman when you feel as if your life is just idling?

No one probably felt like she was in a holding pattern more than Ruth. A barren widow, she willingly followed her also-widowed mother-in-law to a land that was not her own. She didn't know what the future held for her. But she went anyway. It would have been easy to stay behind like her other sister-in-law, but she didn't (Ruth 1:14). Even when she got to Israel, it would have been easy to hide out in Naomi's home. I mean, she was not a native to the country and everyone knew it. Who could blame her if she just chose to sit in a dark room and mourn for a while? But instead she serves Naomi by going to work and providing for her mother-in-law and herself (2:2–7). She didn't know the outcome. She didn't know that through her humble obedience and service the future King of Israel would be born. And isn't that how God works? He takes our humble obedience and turns it into abundant goodness for us and unceasing glory for himself. Ruth did not put her womanhood on hold in her season of limbo. She pressed on in faith, trusting that her faithfulness would serve her bereaved mother-in-law, but also that her faithfulness would yield a harvest for them both.

The ultimate mark of womanhood is hoping in God alone. Of course, this is also the mark of a godly man. But as we look at the lives of saints who have gone before us—such as Ruth, Sarah, Mary, and Elizabeth—we see that though their life circumstances were different, they all had a resolute trust in God alone. They possessed a gentle and quiet spirit that we've talked about, the true beauty that never fades. It's not about giving birth or loving a husband, though these are beautiful and God-glorifying implications of being a woman. But they are not what our identity is rooted in. Whenever we question our value as women, we must always go back to the Bible, rather than listen to the internal voice that is sure to lead us astray.

Where Our Identity Lies

If the ultimate mark of womanhood is a gentle and quiet spirit that hopes in God, then this holds tremendous encouragement for women who long to be wives and mothers. But it holds encouragement for all of us, really. And even if you are not yet thinking about those seasons of life, this applies to you too. God calls us women—created in his image, valuable in his economy, and given a great singular purpose—to display his glory in your specific season, whatever that might be. If you are infertile or unwillingly single, it is not the season you would choose. But it is yours, and it is a gift from God. If you are waiting for your job to take off or finishing school, this is your season designed by God to be used for his glory and your joy. If you wake up every morning wondering how you are going to have the energy to care for your children, God has sufficient grace for you to display his glory in your weakness.

If your marriage is fraught with snide comments and bitter arguments, God is here to meet you in your difficulty. If your job runs you down by the week's end, and you don't know how you'll start again on Monday, God has promised grace for today, tomorrow, and every day after. In our circumstances we can either flourish or wither. We can either hope in God or despise his provision. He has given us everything we need to bear good fruit in our season of life (2 Pet. 1:3–4).

What I had to learn in my years of infertility was that God was meeting my desires to nurture and bear life by giving me classes full of impressionable students. As I taught high school students about God's design for marriage and family, I discovered that I was investing in the lives of the next generation. I was not simply waiting for my life to begin. It was happening right in front of me if only I had eyes to see.

We are not on hold, dear sisters. It might feel like it some days, but God has us exactly where he wants us in our particular season. As women who hope in God, we can bear good fruit for his glory even when our hearts are breaking or our dreams are unfulfilled or dashed again. And that is where our womanhood is most beautifully displayed.

Recovery of the Word

There is, however, something else that must mark you as godly women. As I talked about in the previous chapter, your local church is a place where you should flourish. It is where you should delight to serve and grow in your study of the Word. But your study of the Bible shouldn't be confined within the walls of your churches. It is all well and good to read this book, to listen to sermons on gender, and to talk to your friends about it. But you will never make any lasting progress unless God and his Word grip your own soul, and it won't grip your soul unless you study it for yourself.

Jen Wilkin has these helpful words on the importance of good Bible study methods:

> We must teach the Bible. Please hear me. We must teach the Bible, and we must do so in such a way that those sitting under our teaching learn to feed themselves rather than rely solely on us to feed them. We cannot assume that our people know the first thing about where to start or how to proceed. It is not sufficient to send them a link to a reading plan or a study method. It is our job to give them good tools and to model how to use them.[1]

Biblical women are Word-driven women. They love the Scriptures. They love to study the Scriptures. They want the Bible "stamped on their eyeballs" as Gloria Furman so helpfully says.[2] The only way we are going to turn from feminism is if we know the God of the Bible. The only way we will understand what it means to live fully as his image-bearer is if we know the One whose image we bear. This means that not only do we need to pay careful attention to the type of church we attend, but we also must make every effort to make personal study a priority.

I make time for the things that are important for me. I make time for my kids. I make time for my husband. I make time for my favorite shows. For myself, one barometer for my own spiritual temperature is how much time I'm making for a particular show I'm binge-watching versus how much time I'm making for personal Bible study. It's convicting. But the world is not going to stop throwing punches on the womanhood front so I can finish that next episode. The only ammunition I have against the assault against womanhood is God's inspired and holy Word. The same is true for you, sister. Make time for God's Word. Don't just leave your own spiritual growth up to the Sunday morning sermon. Study God's Word. Read it. Treasure it. It is our very food. It is life-sustaining, if we only open it and delight in it.

Restoration in My Life

As we near the end of this book, I think it's helpful to reiterate that understanding feminism and its influence on us is not about a list of rules. It's not about fitting nicely into a little box or being the perfect wife and mother. We aren't all the same. And there's beauty in those differences. Our womanhood looks different as it manifests itself in each woman. But as I have tried to show throughout the book, while womanhood is not a cookie cutter mold, it is distinctive. It is marked by something profound, something that sets us apart from the women of the world.

Hope in God.

This is what I want you to walk away with—an unwavering hope in the God who created you as a woman. Hope in God is what gives a woman grace to work hard and faithfully in her career. Hope in God is what allows a mother to serve her children when she feels like she just can't make it through another day of tantrums or teenage rebellion. Hope in God is what gives a single woman who desperately longs to be married the resolve to keep going when all prospects seem to have dried up. Hope in God is what sustains a woman who desires children but is staring at another negative pregnancy test. Hope in God is what keeps us in our marriages. It is what keeps us when the storms of life assail us. It is our lifeline. It is what makes us different than the world around us. It's what makes us willing to believe all the Bible teaches about being a godly woman. We aren't turning from feminism because we want to win a battle or prove how right we are. We are turning from feminism because we ultimately want to yield our spirits to the will of the God who created us in his image, for his glory, and with a beautiful and distinct purpose—to display his glory as women.

Study Questions

1. Do you ever feel like a fraud when it comes to being a godly woman? How so? How does the gospel transform your feelings of failure?

2. How is the gospel feminism's greatest foe?

3. What are some ways you can apply a theology of womanhood to your own life right now?

Bibliography

Bessey, Sarah. *Jesus Feminist: An Invitation to Revisit the Bible's View of Women*. New York: Howard, 2013.

Bilzekian, Gilbert. *Beyond Sex Roles: What the Bible Says about a Woman's Place in Church and Family*. Grand Rapids, MI: Baker Academic, 2006.

Dever, Mark. *Nine Marks of a Healthy Church*. Wheaton, IL: Crossway, 2004.

Duncan, J. Ligon and Susan Hunt. *Women's Ministry in the Local Church*. Wheaton, IL: Crossway, 2006.

Friedan, Betty. *The Feminine Mystique*. New York: W. W. Norton, 1963.

Furman, Gloria, *Treasuring Christ When Your Hands Are Full: Gospel Meditations for Busy Moms*. Wheaton, IL: Crossway, 2014.

Grudem, Wayne. *Evangelical Feminism and Biblical Truth: An Analysis of More Than 100 Disputed Questions*. Sisters, OR: Multnomah, 2004.

———. *Systematic Theology: An Introduction to Biblical Doctrine*. Grand Rapids, MI: Zondervan, 1994.

Held Evans, Rachel. *A Year of Biblical Womanhood: How a Liberated Woman Found Herself Sitting on Her Roof, Covering Her Head, and Calling Her Husband "Master."* Nashville, TN: Thomas Nelson, 2012.

Hunt, Susan and Barbara Thompson. *The Legacy of Biblical Womanhood*. Wheaton, IL: Crossway, 2003.

Hymowitz, Kay S. *Manning Up: How the Rise of Women Has Turned Men into Boys*. New York: Basic Books, 2011.

Kassian, Mary. *The Feminist Mistake: The Radical Impact of Feminism on Church and Culture*. Wheaton, IL: Crossway, 2005.

Keller, Tim and Kathy. *The Meaning of Marriage: Facing the Complexities of Commitment with the Wisdom of God*. New York: Dutton, 2011.

Köstenberger, Andreas J. and Thomas R. Schreiner. *Women in the Church: An Analysis and Application of 1 Timothy 2:9–15*. Grand Rapids, MI: Baker Academic, 2005.

Köstenberger, Margaret Elizabeth. *Jesus and the Feminists: Who Do They Say He Is?* Wheaton, IL: Crossway, 2008.

Mahaney, C. J. *Humility: True Greatness*. Colorado Springs, CO: Multnomah, 2005.

Mahaney, Carolyn and Nicole Whitacre. *True Beauty*. Wheaton, IL: Crossway, 2014.

McCulley, Carolyn. *Did I Kiss Marriage Goodbye? Trusting God with a Hope Deferred*. Wheaton, IL: Crossway, 2004.

McCulley, Carolyn and Nora Shank. *The Measure of Success: Uncovering the Biblical Perspective on Women, Work, and the Home*. Nashville, TN: B&H, 2014.

McCulley, Carolyn. *Radical Womanhood: Feminine Faith in a Feminist World*. Chicago: Moody, 2008.

Piper, John. *What's the Difference?: Manhood and Womanhood Defined According to the Bible*. Wheaton, IL: Crossway, 2008.

Valenti, Jessica. *Full Frontal Feminism: A Young Woman's Guide to Why Feminism Matters*. Berkley, CA: Seal Press, 2007.

———. *The Purity Myth: How America's Obsession with Virginity Is Hurting Young Women*. Berkeley, CA: Seal Press, 2009.

Notes

Introduction: I'm an Accidental Feminist

1. Sarah Bessey, *Jesus Feminist: An Invitation to Revisit the Bible's View of Women* (New York: Howard, 2013), 13.
2. Lizzie Crocker, "Why Millennials Think They Hate Feminism," *The Daily Beast,* May 7, 2014, http://www.thedailybeast.com/articles/2014/05/07/why-millennials-think-they-hate-feminism.html.
3. Carolyn McCulley, *Radical Womanhood: Feminine Faith in a Feminist World* (Chicago: Moody, 2008), 34–36.
4. Irving Berlin, "Anything You Can Do," *Annie Get Your Gun,* 1946.

Chapter 1: What It Means to Be a Woman (and not a Man)

1. Betty Friedan, *The Feminine Mystique* (New York: W. W. Norton, 1963), 1–22.
2. Ibid., 70.
3. Ibid., 456.
4. Perry Chiaramonte, "Mr. Mom Era: Stay-at-Home Dads Doubled Over Last Decade," *Fox News,* June 17, 2012, http://www.foxnews.com/us/2012/06/17/mr-mom-era-stay-at-home-dads-doubled-over-last-decade/.
5. Wayne Grudem, *Systematic Theology: An Introduction to Bible Doctrine* (Grand Rapids, MI: Zondervan, 1994), 442.
6. Ibid., 461–62.
7. Susan Hunt and Barbara Thompson, *The Legacy of Biblical Womanhood* (Wheaton, IL: Crossway, 2003), 169.

Chapter 2: What Women Want

1. Andrea Peyser, "Dunst Receives Fury for Feminine Comments in Bazaar," *New York Post,* April 21, 2014, http://nypost.com/2014/04/21/dunst-receives-fury-for-feminine-comments-in-bazaar/.
2. Kay S. Hymowitz, *Manning Up: How the Rise of Women Has Turned Men into Boys* (New York: Basic Books, 2011), 17.
3. Ibid., 151.
4. Ibid., 159.

5. C. J. Mahaney, *Humility: True Greatness* (Colorado Springs, CO: Multnomah, 2005), 98.
6. Susan Hunt and Barbara Thompson, *The Legacy of Biblical Womanhood* (Wheaton, IL: Crossway, 2003), 162.
7. Hymowitz, *Manning Up*, 45.

Chapter 3: Do We Have to Talk about Submission?

1. Philip Delves Broughton, "Marriage at 66 for Radical Feminist Gloria Steinem," *The Telegraph*, September 7, 2007, http://www.telegraph.co.uk/news/worldnews/northamerica/usa/1354464/Marriage-at-66-for-radical-feminist-Gloria-Steinem.html.
2. Yasmine Hafiz, "Candace Cameron Bure Explains Being 'Submissive' to Her Husband," *The Huffington Post*, January 25, 2014, http://www.huffingtonpost.com/2014/01/06/candance-cameron-bure-submissive_n_4550818.html?utm_hp_ref=email_share.
3. See Anna Moeslein, "Zoe Saldana Tells Us about Rosemary's Baby, Making Rosemary a Modern-Day Woman, and More," *Glamour Magazine*, May 10, 2014, http://www.glamour.com/entertainment/blogs/obsessed/2014/05/zoe-saldana-tells-us-about-the.
4. Victoria Murphy, "Kate Middleton Will Not 'Obey' in Royal Wedding Vows—Just Like Prince William's Mum Diana," *The Mirror*, April 22, 2011, http://www.mirror.co.uk/news/uk-news/kate-middleton-will-not-obey-in-royal-124106.
5. Russell Moore, "Women, Stop Submitting to Men," *Moore to the Point*, December 5, 2011, http://www.russellmoore.com/2011/12/05/women-stop-submitting-to-men/.
6. I'm particularly thinking of Gilbert Bilzekian's book *Beyond Sex Roles* (Grand Rapids, MI: Baker Academic, 2006), which argues that the submission talked about in the New Testament is actually a "mutual submission" to one another, not a headship/submission relationship. Others have jumped on this idea as well, but he in particular lays it out in this book. For a different view on this, see Wayne Grudem's *Evangelical Feminism and Biblical Truth* (Sisters, OR: Multnomah, 2004). Grudem examines the idea of "mutual submission" and why this, and other egalitarian arguments, cannot actually be reconciled with the biblical text.

Chapter 4: My Body on Display

1. Sandra Gonzales, "'Girls' Producers Go on 'Rage Spiral' Defending Nudity," *Entertainment Weekly*, January 9, 2014, http://insidetv.ew.com/2014/01/09/girls-producers-defend-nudity/?hpt=hp_t3.
2. Jessica Valenti, *The Purity Myth: How America's Obsession with Virginity Is Hurting Young Women* (Berkeley, CA: Seal Press, 2009), 9, 15.
3. Ibid.
4. Jessica Valenti, *Full Frontal Feminism: A Young Woman's Guide to Why Feminism Matters* (Berkley, CA: Seal Press, 2007), 30.

5. Rachel Held Evans, "Modesty: I Don't Think It Means What You Think It Means," *Q Ideas,* http://www.qideas.org/blog/modesty-i-dont-think-it-means-what-you-think-it-means.aspx.
6. John Piper, "Staying Married Is Not about Staying in Love, Part 2," *Desiring God website,* February 4, 2007, http://www.desiringgod.org/resource-library/sermons/staying-married-is-not-about-staying-in-love-part-2.
7. Tim and Kathy Keller, *The Meaning of Marriage: Facing the Complexities of Commitment with the Wisdom of God* (New York: Dutton, 2011), 223–24.
8. Carolyn Mahaney and Nicole Whitacre, *True Beauty* (Wheaton, IL: Crossway, 2014), 28.
9. See John Keats, "Ode on a Grecian Urn," 1819, www.englishhistory.net/keats/odeonagrecianurn.html/.

Chapter 5: God's Design for the Home

1. "Michelle Obama's Remarks at the Democratic Convention," *New York Times* online, August 25, 2008, http://www.nytimes.com/2008/08/26/us/politics/26text-obama.html?pagewanted=all&_r=0.
2. Lisa Belkin, "The Opt-Out Revolution," *New York Times,* August 7, 2013, http://www.nytimes.com/2013/08/11/magazine/the-opt-out-revolution.html.
3. Judith Warner, "The Opt-Out Generation Wants Back In," *New York Times Magazine,* August 7, 2013, http://www.nytimes.com/2013/08/11/magazine/the-opt-out-generation-wants-back-in.html.
4. Betty Friedan, *The Feminine Mystique* (New York: W.W. Norton, 1963), 22.
5. Rachel Held Evans, *A Year of Biblical Womanhood: How a Liberated Woman Found Herself Sitting on Her Roof, Covering Her Head, and Calling Her Husband "Master"* (Nashville, TN: Thomas Nelson, 2012), 23.
6. Carolyn McCulley and Nora Shank, *The Measure of Success: Uncovering the Biblical Perspective on Women, Work, and the Home* (Nashville, TN: B&H, 2014), 44.
7. Ibid.
8. Carolyn McCulley, *Did I Kiss Marriage Goodbye? Trusting God with a Hope Deferred* (Wheaton, IL: Crossway, 2004), 108.
9. McCulley and Shank, *The Measure of Success.*

Chapter 6: Women in the Church

1. Mark Dever, *Nine Marks of a Healthy Church* (Wheaton, IL: Crossway, 2004), 31–32.
2. Ligon Duncan and Susan Hunt, *Women's Ministry in the Local Church* (Wheaton, IL: Crossway, 2006), 48–49.
3. Wayne Grudem, *Systematic Theology: An Introduction to Biblical Doctrine* (Grand Rapids, MI: Zondervan, 1994), 940.

4. Fabs Harford, "It's Time to Speak," *Thoughts from Fabs* (blog), January 4, 2013, http://www.fabsharford.com/its-time-to-speak/.
5. For a more thorough list of the many ways women can serve in the church, see John Piper, *What's the Difference: Manhood and Womanhood Defined According to the Bible* (Wheaton, IL: Crossway, 2008). I'm thinking particularly of the helpful chart on pages 80–81. While the list isn't exhaustive, it is something to help you start thinking through these issues.
6. Margaret Elizabeth Köstenberger, *Jesus and the Feminists: Who Do They Say He Is?* (Wheaton, IL: Crossway, 2008), 19–20.
7. Ibid, 20.
8. The topic of women being silent in the context of 1 Timothy 2:9–15 is complex and beyond the scope of this book. In fact, entire books have been written about this passage alone. For a more in-depth study of Paul's meaning and context for this passage see Andreas Köstenberger and Thomas R. Schreiner, *Women in the Church: An Analysis and Application of 1 Timothy 2:9–15* (Grand Rapids, MI: Baker Academic, 2005).
9. Mary Kassian, *The Feminist Mistake: The Radical Impact of Feminism on Church and Culture* (Wheaton, IL: Crossway, 2005), 287–88.
10. John Piper, "Don't Waste Your Life," Campus Crusade Christmas Conference, December 29, 2003, http://www.desiringgod.org/conference-messages/dont-waste-your-life--2.

Chapter 7: Restoration Is Possible

1. Jen Wilkin, "The Assumption We Cannot Afford," *The Beginning of Wisdom* (blog), April 13, 2014, http://jenwilkin.blogspot.com/2014/04/the-assumption-we-cannot-afford.html.
2. Gloria Furman, *Treasuring Christ When Your Hands Are Full: Gospel Meditations for Busy Moms* (Wheaton, IL: Crossway, 2014), 13–22.

General Index

Scripture Index